Sōsh: Improving Social Skills with Children and Adolescents

Sōsh: Improving Social Skills with Children and Adolescents

Mark Bowers, Ph.D.

Edited by

Kelly M. Bowers, Ph.D.

ISBN: 978-0-578-08432-9 Paperback

Printed in the United States of America

For more information, contact:

Mark Bowers, Ph.D., PLLC

1601 Briarwood Circle, Suite 500

Ann Arbor, MI 48108

www.mysosh.com

www.aacenter.org

The pronoun "he" is used throughout this book to avoid using "he or
she," however all information contained in this book was included with
both females and males in mind.

to Kelly and the kids

Table of Contents

Chapter One

Introduction

Introduction

Meet Justin. He is 15 years old and has been working to improve his social skills since he was 6 years old, when he was first identified by a psychologist as having delayed social skills. His parents have been very supportive, enrolling him in social skills groups, taking him to therapy appointments, arranging play dates, and seeking assistance from his schools for nearly ten years. Justin is academically gifted and his high school continues to assert that as long as his grades continue to be straight "A's" there is no justification for assisting with his social development. As smart as Justin is, he now refuses to attend school. His parents have a number of hypotheses about his refusal to attend school but he tells his parents, "It just doesn't make sense to go." His parents wonder if the recent increase in peer-intensive interactions, such as a recent school camp outing without adequate support from the school, has been stressful for Justin.

He appears to be depressed. He is quiet during his therapy sessions and social groups because he feels he isn't making progress. He would rather sleep or create a virtual identity for himself on his computer than interact with others. Specifically, most of his time is spent building an avatar of himself on the computer where he is able to "escape" the reality of his situation and focus on how his life "could be" through the computer. His parents created a daily schedule for him and are encouraging him to follow it. This way, at least he is doing *something* even though he is not attending school. The family wonders when they might be contacted by a truancy officer. The school expects him to return and believes that his school refusal is a manipulative attempt by Justin because of how smart he is. Indeed, the school believes he simply does not want to do any work. Why did all of the time and effort in therapy not pay off? What could the school have done differently to improve Justin's situation? How can the family approach Justin now that he is refusing school so that he can finish his education and achieve his goals for the future? These are the questions that will be addressed in this book. These are the issues central to Sōsh™.

I developed the Sōsh approach and wrote this book in response to my own professional frustration regarding the difficulty children experience when attempting to execute and generalize strategies "taught" to them in social skills groups or during individual counseling sessions. As I have narrowed my professional focus over the years to social skills difficulties, and the various diagnostic presentations that often result in these difficulties, I am disappointed. Indeed, I eagerly read new social skills training methodologies, but remain puzzled at the persistent attempt to teach direct skills through rote learning (e.g., "Look me in the eye!") and in solely superficial environments (e.g., therapy offices). Every parent wants their child to be social and to have friends. The problem is that practitioners have yet to fully understand how to accomplish these goals when a child lacks natural abilities in the social domain.

My favorite definition of social skills is simple: Social skills are specific behaviors used in social situations to produce *desirable* social outcomes (McFall, 1982). Social skills are critical to having success in both childhood and adulthood. In order to develop and improve these skills, you have to utilize them. Think about how often and in how many domains you use social skills every day. You have opportunities all the time. These opportunities are *essential* to develop conversational skills, problem-solving, perspective-taking, and emotional control. This presents a Catch-22 for the individual who struggles with social skills.

This person needs to interact with others in order to improve social functioning, but does not yet know how to effectively do so. How do we help this person develop his social skills? To understand how to help, let's briefly review the science related to social skills treatment.

Social skills are very difficult to study due to the fact that they are often taught in superficial settings and therefore lack generalizability to "real" social settings. The available research regarding how to improve social skills is not promising. White, Keonig, and Scahill (2007) noted that social skills difficulties only get worse with age as the social demands increase and social interactions become more confusing and complicated. The data from their research indicate that children with social difficulties who are included in general education classrooms experience more rejection and isolation, while children in special education settings lack exposure to appropriate peer modeling necessary to improve social function. The authors also identified that social skills deficits contribute to academic and occupational underachievement and eventually to mood and anxiety difficulties. The implications for this are tremendous, especially when trying to advocate for social skills assistance during the school day for a child like Justin, who may be doing well academically. When a school tells a parent concerned about social skills development that their child "is doing fine academically," the response should be that it is only a matter of time before the child's deficits in social skills *will* affect his academics. He may even become depressed or anxious in the absence of the necessary supports. If the school does not believe this or accuses you of trying to predict the future, it may be useful to reference this research to support your assertion.

To be fair regarding the apparent ineffectiveness of social skills interventions, the research literature on social groups and social skills treatment approaches is still in its infancy (White et al., 2007). So far, much of the research on social skills training has been based on the observations of clinicians, educators, or other practitioners who implemented a specific social skills intervention with a small number of children, later evaluating its effectiveness. Researchers are attempting to identify common problems or limitations in current approaches, highlight promising strategies, and make recommendations for future research.

Unfortunately, when formalized social skills programs have been examined as a comprehensive body of research, evaluation of their usefulness has not always been encouraging. After reviewing 55 research studies on school-based social skills programs for children with Autism, for example, Bellini, Peters, Benner, and Hopf (2007) found such programs to be only minimally effective. They identified major problems with existing programs including low dosage (the children did not receive many hours of social skills training). This makes it evident that, due to its complexity, social skills development requires significant time devoted to practice and teaching.

Another issue identified was the need to conduct the intervention in the child's natural setting, such as the classroom, rather than in a "pull-out" setting (e.g., a therapy session in a clinician's office or in a school resource room). Indeed, treatment in naturalistic settings appears to be more effective (Bellini et al., 2007). Thus, the more coaching and support that children receive during natural, daily interactions, the more positive their social outcomes. Schools often create scenarios intended to increase social skills, such as a resource room "social group" where peers are encouraged to have discussions or play games. These interactions, however, can be superficial due to their "scripted" nature, such as providing topics for discussion. Therefore any skills acquired may not generalize well to everyday interactions in the absence of the group leader who prompts for a particular response. Also noted in the research (Bellini et al., 2007) is the need to focus on making sure skills are generalized, that is, used in other contexts. Ensuring that new social skills are practiced and used far beyond the clinic or even the school setting is crucial to a social skills training program's success.

A common problem with social skills research is the amount of participants involved is often very small, and studies evaluating the effectiveness of the intervention are not "masked" to prevent any biases of raters from influencing their assessment of the program's worth (i.e., people rating their own studies or treatment approach may rate them as more successful). Further, few of the studies used comparison groups that would allow researchers to distinguish improvement due to an intervention, versus improvement due to the person's natural course of development and maturation. In other words, how many of the children who improved would have done so anyway despite their participation in a social skills treatment group? Finally, few studies involved follow-up, in the short or long term, to see if any of the skills gained were retained (Rao, Beidel, & Murray, 2008).

On a positive note, researchers looking at social skills efforts have identified several elements that seem to contribute to a worthwhile social skills program. Williams et al. (2007) reviewed 14 studies, and identified a number of "promising strategies":

- Increase social motivation (foster self-awareness and self-esteem; develop a fun and nurturing environment).
- Increase social initiations (exercise strategies to initiate interactions and make social rules concrete. For example, "Stay one arm's length away from the other person").

- Improve appropriate social responding (use modeling and role-playing to teach skills).

- Reduce interfering behaviors such as tantrums or personal space invasion (reinforce positive behaviors by, for example, maintaining behavior charts and reinforcing desired behavior with stars).

- Promote skill generalization by orchestrating peer involvement, using multiple trainers, involving parents in training, providing opportunities to practice skills in naturalistic settings, and assigning "homework" -- having children practice between sessions.

Another key issue for social skills development is the need for interventions to require not only interacting with other people, but as many different kinds of people as possible. One-on-one direct teaching or therapy is important to social skills training, but to truly practice a social skill requires creating a social situation or utilizing a preexisting one. The more a person practices and the more people he practices with, the greater his likelihood of improving skills. This point applies to learning in general. The more that a person uses and practices newly acquired knowledge in a variety of contexts, the more ingrained this knowledge and skill set becomes.

Matson, Matson, and Rivet (2007) completed an evaluation of numerous social interventions (79 studies in all) for children with social difficulties, with participants who displayed a wide range of functioning in other areas of development (e.g., language, intelligence). Despite some wide-ranging individual differences, the authors suggested that effective intervention programs include the following:

- Parent training and education so that intervention can occur for younger children with the goal of improving skills and generalization to various settings.

- Treatment to address interfering behaviors or emotions such as disruptive behaviors or anxiety.

- Early start (the younger the identification of difficulty the better).

- Social skills must be practiced and coached while in the school setting.

- Differentiation and accommodation of the child's needs within the approach (i.e., address basic versus more advanced skill development needs).

- Consistent use of some sort of quantifiable rating scale to assess if children are meeting their specific goals over time.

Thus, an effective social skills program should include a number of variables, many of which seem like common sense. Certainly, it is easy to assume that the more you practice (with a variety of people and in a variety of locations), the more that you promote success. However, there are other variables identified in the research literature that remain out of many families' control. These include providing social skills instruction, modeling, and coaching in the general education classroom or school setting such as a lunch room or playground. The age at which a family begins intervention is also important and, as with most things in life, the sooner you begin the better. However, as you will learn with the Sōsh approach, what you do with the child while they are young (birth through 8 years) *is important* as it lays a necessary developmental foundation, but children are not fully invested in making social improvements until they are in the third or fourth grade. Finally, addressing behavioral or emotional issues associated with social skills difficulties may require assistance from a child specialist. The Sōsh methodology outlines a variety of strategies to improve functioning in these areas, but consultation with a qualified developmental specialist with expertise in social skills is strongly encouraged.

What is Sōsh?

Acknowledging that social skills research is still in its infancy, researchers are offering recommendations for next steps. Some useful techniques and tools have been created and now need to be refined. The most effective approach identified by researchers (Matson et al., 2007) is a combination of: 1) promoting skill generalization by orchestrating peer involvement, 2) using multiple trainers, 3) involving parents in training, 4) providing opportunities to practice skills in naturalistic settings, and 5) assigning "homework" (i.e., having children practice between sessions). This set of critical treatment variables is the foundation of the Sōsh philosophy.

The Sōsh approach to social skills improvement is based on more than a decade of work with children, adolescents, and young adults who struggle with social difficulties. The Sōsh framework divides social functioning into five areas essential to social skills development and success: **Relate** (Connect with Others), **Relax** (Reduce Stress), **Regulate** (Manage Behaviors), **Reason** (Think it Through) and **Recognize** (Understand Feelings). These "**5 R's**" serve as a road map for individuals who want to be social, but have faced obstacles in the past or don't know how or where to begin. Sōsh also serves as a guide for parents, teachers, and therapists hoping to encourage and assist individuals with their social goals. Just as parents are learning how to assist their children with social skills, many teachers and therapists are not well-versed in this area despite being skilled in their respective professions in general. With exercises, strategies and information for home, school, and even therapy settings, Sōsh will help guide you and your child, student, or client every step of the way.

The goal of Sōsh is to provide individuals and families, as well as schools and therapists, with a powerful interactive technological tool (the mobile application) in combination with a practical description of social skills strategies (the book) to help children improve their social interactions and relationships. The hope is that having this book, with examples and strategies from my everyday work with children, will help parents to avoid and, if needed, break unhealthy habits while supporting and challenging their children to try out social situations and create new habits that promote connections with others.

The idea for the Sōsh approach grew out of my repeated observations that an individual's innate understanding and self-awareness of social interactions is often lacking. Indeed, during my work with children, adolescents, and young adults I find that trying to teach social skills to someone who is unaware of their current patterns is futile. Beyond a lack of interest, we often try to teach social skills to a child who does not yet have the developmental capacity to learn such skills. Certainly, you wouldn't take a toddler to their first swimming lesson, throw them in the pool and yell "swim!" from the sideline. You would ease them into the water, let them get comfortable, warm up, and work on a few specific skills (e.g., kicking legs while holding onto the wall or a kick board) until the next lesson, where you would review these skills and build on them with more complex movements. Thus, an effective approach to social skills must involve a full understanding and consideration of the child's developmental capacity in order to tailor the approach accordingly.

The Sōsh mobile application travels with children, teens, and young adults when they need it the most: *In the moment.* This is consistent with the aforementioned research that stresses the importance of live, real world interactions and coaching to improve social skills. The Sōsh mobile app provides the means necessary for an individual to study his style of interaction, document it, and it also includes a wealth of tools and strategies to be used in anticipation of, or in response to, daily social exchanges and challenges. Further, parents often ask, "Where do I begin to help my child?" The answer to this can usually be found by observing how the child's peers interact with each other and then comparing that to how the child is relating to his peers. Individuals with social skills difficulties need to observe their peers and gather information regarding how to appropriately interact. The Sōsh mobile app allows a person to collect data during peer observations and interactions, and practice specific skills at a developmentally appropriate pace while also encouraging continued and repeated use of the strategies. The user is even able to "prove" their use of the app to an interested parent or therapist by archiving data. They can share a PDF file of the day's progress and notes with the family, school, or therapist who can reward their efforts accordingly (e.g., 15 extra minutes of a fun activity at home for each daily archive turned in).

Further, the mobile app is designed with schools in mind so elementary through college-age students can use this technology throughout their school day, when many social opportunities and challenges arise. The Sōsh application functionality is based on my desire to be with the child during their day to provide coaching and assistance. During my counseling sessions with families in my private practice, I hear about many missed opportunities or mistakes made during a child's daily interactions and I have often said to myself, "I wish I could have been there to coach." By developing this technology, now I *can* be. The strategies that I tell children to practice are organized and contained within the mobile app that they take with them wherever they go. This helps to alleviate stress regarding where to begin or how to practice these skills. When adults can't be with the child to assist them and coach them, the Sōsh mobile app can.

The Sōsh approach can also help schools answer the question, "What do we do to help this child?" Whether school staff reads the book, uses the mobile application, or both, they can now have the tools to assist them. Further, if schools assert that a child does not need formalized assistance such as an Individualized Education Program (IEP) or Section 504 Plan (to be discussed further in the **Sōsh in Schools** chapter), the mobile app can be supplied by the family. Therefore, the school does not incur any expense associated with helping the child. The school simply allows the child to use the Sōsh app during the school day to aid in their development (which does require creating some parameters around how the child uses the device in school so that it is not a distraction).

Dovetailing with the features of the mobile application is a built-in community (www.mysosh.com) of Sōsh mobile application users. Each user of the mobile app receives an access code to the Members Only section of the website where everyone has the same goal: Help improve social skills. Members can share ideas and strategies. This exclusive section of the website also includes message boards on all topics related to Sōsh as well as social skills and human development in general. The website also provides video modeling examples and encourages member video submissions demonstrating successful approaches. If members allow, these videos can be uploaded to the Media section of the Sōsh mobile app by individual users so that kids can watch video models of other children successfully engaging in a social skill that they are working on. In addition, there is a newsfeed of the latest science and news related to social development as well as an up-to-date resources library. This site is maintained by me, with the assistance of another licensed psychologist. We regularly contribute and respond to message board comments and queries. Finally, we provide periodic webinars to share tips and techniques, discuss research, and provide support to members who are working with a child, client, student, or loved one. This community is encouraged to provide feedback regarding the features of the mobile application so that future updated versions will be as user-friendly and helpful as possible.

Who Is It For?

The Sōsh approach described throughout this book is ideal for individuals who want assistance improving their social skills and for the parents, teachers, and therapists who want to help them. The Sōsh mobile application is designed for individuals ages eight and older (i.e., early 30's), although parents of younger children (i.e., toddler through school age) find the strategies contained in the app useful to guide their approach. This book is written as a parent's guide so the term "child" is used throughout. The pronoun "he" is used throughout the book to avoid using "he or she;" however, everything in this book can be used by parents of both girls and boys. This book is intended to compliment children using the Sōsh mobile app so that parents also have a "map" of how to proceed and guide their child's social skills progress. For older teens and young adults, they can begin by using the app, and any adults working with them may benefit from reading the book as well. Parents of children using the mobile app are strongly encouraged to read this text. Individual creativity with the mobile app strategies is encouraged as the technology is designed to help make each individual treatment customized.

Many children with social difficulties are diagnosed with a neurodevelopmental disorder, or disorder of neural development, which is an impairment of the growth and development of the brain or central nervous system that affects emotion and learning. Having a neurodevelopmental disorder affects development, and at the same time developmental changes have an effect on the degree that a neurodevelopmental disorder is expressed.

Disorders considered to be neurodevelopmental in origin, or to have neurodevelopmental consequences when they occur during infancy or childhood, include Autism and Autism Spectrum Disorders such as Pervasive Developmental Disorder-Not Otherwise Specified (PDD-NOS), Asperger's Syndrome, Attention-Deficit Disorders, Learning Disabilities such as Dyslexia and Nonverbal Learning Disorder, Traumatic Brain Injury, and genetic disorders such as Fragile X and Prader-Willi Syndrome. Neurodevelopmental diagnoses are associated with widely varying degrees of social, cognitive, emotional, physical, and sensory difficulties for individuals, families and society in general.

Trying to address social difficulties in a child with a neurodevelopmental diagnosis requires expertise in both social functioning and ancillary factors which accompany the overall profile (e.g., sensory, behavioral concerns). Difficulty locating a treatment provider with expertise in these issues can be a barrier to social progress for many families and their children. Thus, the Sōsh approach and mobile app can help many families who need guidance, but they are also urged to identify a professional to guide them. The Sōsh approach is ideally used in the moment with periodic check-ins with a developmental treatment provider.

Sōsh is a comprehensive set of strategies and recommendations that families with whom I have counseled have found success. I want to now pass these strategies along to you and your family. Sōsh is a useful tool for any individual experiencing social difficulties, regardless of the reason or whether or not the individual has a formal medical or psychological diagnosis. I hope that you find the Sōsh approach to be your solution to help improve your child's social skills.

Chapter Two

Understanding Development:

The Windows

Understanding Development: The Windows

Every parent needs to have a basic understanding of child development in order to assist their child with social difficulties. There is no need to memorize this information, but rather you should review the information as questions arise. It may be useful to consider development from various specific theoretical perspectives, two of which are outlined in this chapter.

There is one important neurodevelopmental factor that I cannot stress enough: Each and every time you experience *sustained* gains in any area of social functioning, another stage of development will begin. You certainly deserve to pat yourself (and your child) on the back for making it this far; however, your child will wake up, seemingly the very next day, and begin to experience a new set of difficulties related to a new stage of their development. It is critical that at these transitional times or stages the child's presentation not be interpreted as regression. Indeed, new challenges are often misinterpreted as new delays. Certainly the gains that you and your child have made up to that point will contribute to the ease with which you approach and complete the next stage of development. So view this change not as a "setback" but as a marker of success, and don't panic or start to give up! Recharge your energy if needed, keep humor and affect high, and keep the creativity in your approach flowing.

One of the most difficult aspects of social skills work, beyond how much persistence and effort is required, is the need to alter the approach according to how the child is progressing through each stage of development. Further, it is essential to remember that a child's *chronological* age is based on birth date, but a child's *developmental* age is based on progress through anticipated stages of development, which will be covered in this chapter. So while a child may be expected to progress through a certain stage when they are chronologically six years old, for example, they may need assistance with developmental tasks, such as social interactions, that most four or five year-olds can complete. If you prepare yourself and keep this book as a reference, then you will alleviate a lot of stress associated with where you think your child should be developmentally compared to where they actually are. It is essential to work with a child at their current *developmental* stage in order to make social gains. I encourage you to use the information about each stage to determine whether your child is developmentally progressing through a stage, regardless of his chronological age. If a child gets "pushed" to move forward into the next stage of development without having achieved the necessary foundation in prior areas of development, further progress will not be supported, the child will become stuck, and you will become frustrated.

Sōsh is a developmental approach that considers a person's social development across the lifespan and draws on the work of two developmental theorists, Jean Piaget and Erik Erikson, to inform what to expect from children during each stage of development. Piaget focused on cognitive development while Erikson was interested in how children socialize and how this affects their sense of self. Both of these theories are essential to understanding how to help a child make improvements in social functioning.

Probably the most cited theorist regarding the cognitive development of children is Jean Piaget. As with all stage theories, Piaget's *Origins of Intelligence in Children* (1952) maintains that children go through specific stages as their intellect and ability matures. Children start with rudimentary interactions such as grabbing and mouthing objects and eventually progress to highly sophisticated skills such as scientific observation. A chief tenet of Piaget's theory, consistent with the Sōsh approach, is that these stages do not vary in order, cannot be skipped, and should not be rushed. The age range for each stage, however, can vary from child to child. Thus, do your best to determine if your child is developing according to the chronological age markers specific to each of Piaget's stages as covered below or whether there are developmental gaps that place the child within an earlier stage of development. Piaget's work in child cognition has revolutionized science's way of thinking not only about children, but about learning, intelligence, and the nature of knowledge. His work serves as a powerful tool to help understand how to teach a child social skills based on his current stage of development.

Cognitive Development (Piaget)

Sensorimotor Stage: Birth - 2 Years

During this stage, the child learns about himself and his environment through motor and reflex actions. The child interacts with his environment using physical means (sucking, pushing, grabbing, and shaking). These interactions build the child's cognitive brain structures that aid him in understanding and interpreting the world and its functions as well as how to respond to the physical overtures of others. Object permanence is discovered (i.e., things still exist while out of view, such as putting a ball behind your back and the child crawls around you to get it). Teaching a child during this stage is best accomplished via the senses (i.e., vision, hearing, touch, smell, and taste). You can modify behavior by using the senses such as a frown (visual senses) or a stern voice (auditory senses) to alert a child to their inappropriate behavior (e.g., saying "No" in a firm voice while demonstrating a furrowed brow in response to a 12-month-old biting you on the shoulder during a hug). Further, the way that you initially begin to connect with your child, other than talking to him, is to physically play with and hold him.

What we know about play from the very earliest stages, whether we look at this in the animal behavior literature or among human beings, is that we play using our *bodies* initially (Brown & Vaughan, 2010). Through physical play, brain development is improved as well as our relationships with each other. We make our first contact and connection with one another via physical means. Infants grab at objects as they begin to develop. They roll on their stomachs. They hold their head up. They crawl. They have innate reflexes that allow them to feel the sensation of falling and they have depth perception. The Moro reflex, for example, is a hard-wired startle response that, from birth, results in the infant responding with physical movement and even crying in response to loud noises or the sensation of falling. They begin to explore the world for its sensory properties, often by putting objects in their mouths.

Infants enjoy bodily physical play which includes having their faces covered with a blanket and then pulled away in a game of peek-a-boo, being tossed in the air, or having "raspberries" blown on their bellies. These are examples of the ways we first connect and bond with one another from a social standpoint. Thus, our initial social overtures with children are physical in nature and involve bodily interactions given that language is not yet present. Although we talk to our children to model language, we also model interactions with each other through our play. For example, sharing is modeled when we roll a ball on the ground and then pass it to the child so that he can have a turn to roll it. We might also clap together when we sing or listen to songs, or to cheer on a particular behavior.

Preoperational Stage: 18 months - 7 Years

This is the stage in which most children begin to talk. Some children who are at-risk for experiencing social difficulties may experience language delays. The child who is beginning to speak during the early stages of this developmental window applies his new knowledge of language and uses symbols to represent objects or themes. Thus, pretend play emerges with toys used both for their intended purposes as well as their imaginary value (e.g., a toy car can "drive" on the road as expected, but can also fly through the air like a spaceship as the child makes rocket noises). The child is better able to think about things and events that are not immediately present (e.g., "I have that toy at home!").

Oriented to the present, the child has difficulty conceptualizing time. Trying to discuss plans in advance such as what will happen next week, or understanding how much time remains following a 5-minute transition warning, is nearly impossible for this child. His thinking is influenced by fantasy, the way he would like things to be, and he assumes that others see situations from his viewpoint. Thus, perspective-taking is difficult.

The child is not yet able to form abstract conceptions, and must have hands-on, in-the-moment experiences in order to form basic conclusions. Typically, experiences must occur repeatedly before the child grasps the cause-and-effect connection. This is why behavioral modification requires repeated efforts, and also why many parents believe that their behavioral attempts are "not working" when the child does not quickly respond. Repetition of all teaching moments is necessary for learning to occur, no matter how "intelligent" the child.

The more that you teach this child *in the moment*, the more ingrained the learning will be and the greater the likelihood that these lessons will generalize to other situations. Knowing that children during this stage of development learn best from hands-on experiences, putting them in social interactions, as opposed to just talking about social skills, is necessary for improvement to occur. This is consistent with the research findings that indicate practice and exposure in real-world scenarios lead to better gains in social skills (Bellini et al., 2007). Further, exposing a child to novel situations with a variety of kids (with whom they can practice new and recently familiar skills) promotes generalization. Thus, when your child begins to spontaneously share during a play date at home with a familiar friend, you want to praise and reward this behavior. You could then take the child to a public location or play group and look for an opportunity to reward him again for using the sharing behavior in a new context that involves different, and perhaps unfamiliar, kids.

Concrete Stage: 7-12 Years

During this stage the child develops an ability to think abstractly and to make rational judgments about concrete or observable phenomena, which in the past he needed to touch and manipulate physically in order to understand. When teaching this child, giving him the opportunity to ask questions and to explain things back to you allows him to mentally manipulate information. Thinking becomes less self-centered and the child can now account for the perspectives of others. The child attempts more sophisticated explanations and predictions for events. He engages in abstract problem-solving such as mental math, but still understands best when educational material refers to real-life situations. Children who are mentally inflexible and have difficulty with perspective-taking begin to experience increased challenges while trying to interact with their peer group during this stage. Play remains an important aspect of interpersonal functioning and relationship development.

The Importance of Play

Perhaps the definition of the word "play" changes as we get older, but as we mature and develop the amount of time in which we are engaged in play should remain constant. As young adults grow older and become parents, hopefully they evolve into the type of parents who want to play with their children, which will encourage the cycle of play to continue through generations. Play is more than just fun, it promotes creativity, it encourages problem-solving, and it improves relationships.

If you are reading this book and you are the parent of an older child, the importance of play applies equally, although the content and the quality of pretend play is certainly dramatically different among younger children than it is among middle school children, teens, and young adults. At a very early age, we learn about our world and our social environment by watching/modeling our parents and through our play. Regarding the latter, adults and children play differently in some ways, but they play similarly in many other ways. Many of us are reminded how similar our approach to play can be when we have our own children. With young boys, for example, many parents engage in rough-and-tumble play. It comes naturally and easily to both parties and is mutually enjoyed. Something starts to change in our own body chemistry and emotional status as we are playing this way: We connect with the child on a deeper level than if we just sat and watched the child play. The noticeable effect of this approach is that you begin to feel young again yourself, you bond with your child, and your mood improves from the physical exercise involved in this type of play.

Try your best not to become too stressed or focused, initially, on the *quality* and *content* of the play with a child. Your primary objectives are: 1) Put in the time. Parents should play with kids whenever the opportunity presents itself (and work to create the opportunities if they don't present themselves enough!), and 2) Have fun. If you are genuinely concerned that you don't play "well" as a parent, then seek out some guidance. Most play therapy training in psychology is simply about following the child's lead, helping him to build on his ideas and have more fun, and commenting on what he is doing rather than asking him questions. You want to play with your child as much as possible because through play the child solves problems, generates ideas, and works through dilemmas in a safe and socially acceptable manner. It may be easier for some children to use action figures or puppets to resolve real life conflicts than it would be for them to address the same issues from their own perspective. If you are in search of a thorough analysis of the importance of play, I highly recommend Sandra Russ's book, *Play in Child Development*.

Formal Operations: 12 Years - Adulthood

This is the final stage of cognitive development that extends throughout the adult years. The individual no longer requires physical/tangible objects to make rational judgments. At this point, he is capable of hypothetical and deductive reasoning. Teaching approaches for the adolescent may be wide ranging because the child is able to consider many possibilities from several perspectives. Thinking becomes more abstract, incorporating the principles of formal logic.

As children grow older, the focus tends to shift from what I do when I'm playing with others ("hanging out") to who I play (or "hang out") with. Play becomes more focused on relationships as opposed to topics of interest. Play remains just as important at this stage. Indeed, teenagers are quite skilled at playing with ideas even though parents and teachers may not always agree with their ideas, or may not think they are realistic in their approach to solving the world's dilemmas. It remains important, nonetheless, that we allow adolescents this cognitive flexibility to be able to "play" with their ideas.

As adults we can model for kids that playing is fun and that there is always time and opportunity for play. Adults can find ways to play in conjunction with family life whether it's taking on a hobby or coaching Little League. Play changes in structure, shape, and form as we age but the benefits remain. The amazing thing about play is that it is fun, kids love it, and playing as an adult not only helps improve your relationships with your kids, but it also lowers stress so that you have the energy needed to get through your day.

Psychosocial Development (Erikson)

Like Piaget, Erik Erikson maintained that a child's development occurs in a predetermined order. Instead of focusing on cognitive development, however, Erikson was interested in how children socialize and how this affects their sense of self. Erikson's life-stage virtues (1963) consist of eight distinct stages, each with two possible outcomes. For example, progression through one stage referred to as *Industry versus Inferiority* results in the person either becoming *industrious* (learning or developing new skills) or feeling *inferior* (feeling incompetent or like a failure). According to the theory, successful completion of each stage results in healthy personality development and successful interactions with others. Failure to successfully complete a stage can result in a reduced ability to complete further stages and a diminished sense of self, resulting in lowered self-esteem. These stages, however, can be resolved successfully at a later time. Like Erikson's theory, the Sōsh approach maintains that a person must experience success in <u>all</u> of the "**5 R's**" (i.e., **Relate, Relax, Reason, Regulate**, and **Recognize**) to truly make progress in social development.

Infancy: Birth - 18 Months

Erikson referred to infancy as the period of development in which the adult focus is on positive and loving care for the child, with a strong emphasis on visual contact and touch. This is consistent with Piaget's theory during this stage of development which emphasizes the importance of physical contact with the child for bonding and learning to occur. For a child to pass successfully through this period of development, they must learn to trust that life is generally comfortable and have basic confidence in the future. If the child fails to experience trust and is constantly frustrated because his needs are not met, then he may end up with a deep-seated sense of worthlessness and a mistrust of the world in general. The question is whether or not the child determines that his caregivers are reliable and that the caregivers consistently respond to his needs. Thus, social, intellectual, and emotional development begins at birth and is significantly dependent on how our caregivers respond to and interact with us.

Early Childhood: 18 Months - 3 Years

During this stage children learn to master skills by themselves. Not only do they learn to walk, talk, and feed themselves during this time; children also learn fine motor development as well as toilet training. Children are working to build self-esteem and autonomy as they gain more control over their bodies and acquire new skills, such as learning right from wrong. One of the child's newfound skills during the "Terrible

Two's" is the ability to use the powerful word, "No!" It may be frustrating for parents, but it develops important skills of the will. This may sound strange, but there may be cause for concern if the child is *not* opinionated or if the child is overly agreeable or willing to just sit back and watch during this stage. Children with social difficulties tend to remain in the social periphery as active observers or passive "interacters" (i.e., continuing to play but not with others), or appear disinterested in other children during the first three years of life. Parallel play is still acceptable although 2-3 year-olds begin to have brief and even sustained reciprocal interactions with each other. However, not referencing other children at all is always cause for concern. Even children as young as ten months will crawl to another child at one point or another when they are in the same room. Children who enter a playroom at this stage and are only interested in the toys without at least some regard for the other kids may be at-risk for experiencing social difficulties.

It is also during this stage, however, that kids can feel vulnerable from an emotional standpoint. If a child is embarrassed or shamed while learning important skills, as sometimes occurs in the process of toilet training, for example, the child can doubt his capabilities and suffer low self-esteem as a result. An example of this would be scolding a child for having an overnight wetting accident during toilet training or for missing the toilet during urination. Thus, parents and caregivers must strike up an appropriate balance of patience and understanding while also encouraging the child to approach new aspects of their development, especially in the area of social interactions. A child may present as shy or nervous, and even avoidant due to feelings of vulnerability secondary to not knowing how to interact with others. Having a trusted and supportive adult in the environment to facilitate interactions can alleviate much of this stress and encourage future, repeated attempts.

The most significant relationships are with parents during this time. Although adults may begin referring to other children as "friends" of the child, the primary social interactions still come from mom and dad. The child needs encouragement and support exploring the world, especially while he is pursuing social relationships.

Play Age: 3 - 5 Years

During this stage of development, children experience a desire to mimic or copy the adults around them and take initiative in creating play situations with adults as well as other children. Children make up stories with dolls, talk into toy phones, make engine noises with miniature cars or animal noises with animal toys, and experiment with "grown up" life via role plays and dress up. Children also begin to use that wonderful question for exploring the world that often has adults stumped: "Why?" Formal early childhood education begins during this stage and utilizes play as the first approach to teaching children.

The most significant relationships during these years are with the immediate family. Thus, the primary play partners continue to be parents and siblings, but families are strongly encouraged to expand the child's playmates to neighbors, children of friends, and peers that the child meets during activities, play groups, or early education programs. This is consistent with the social skills research discussed in the **Introduction** chapter that recommends variety among the people that a child interacts with. The "danger" associated with interactions around highly familiar children such as siblings or relatives is that these interactions become comfortable and repetitive over time. Exposure to varied groups of children, situations, and environments is essential for overall social skills success.

School Age: 6 - 12 Years

During this stage, that concludes with the so-called 'tween years, a child is capable of learning, creating, and accomplishing numerous new skills and knowledge, thus developing a sense of industry. The child begins to identify more strongly with the parent of the same sex and has increased interest in friends of the same sex, participation in clubs, and hero/role-model figures (e.g., professional athletes, pop stars, teen idols). Children during this stage have wonderful entrepreneurial ideas that, with proper adult supervision and support, not only boost self-esteem but can also generate some spending money. Consider a 9-year-old girl who not only has a dog walking business but also makes cakes (with the help of her mom) and has business cards and regular customers for *both* of her business ventures!

This is also a very social stage of development, and if unresolved feelings of inadequacy and inferiority are experienced the child can have serious problems with competence and self-esteem. A central component of Sōsh is what I term the social "switch" that seems to turn on in a child's brain around his ninth birthday. This is the time in which the child reports more interest in having friends and social interactions. For the child with social skills difficulties, this can be a frustrating and stressful time given that the desire to connect is now active but the skills needed for successful connection remain dormant or do not yet exist. Thus, parents, teachers, caregivers, therapists (if applicable), and the child need to be prepared for this time with a variety of strategies so that self-esteem can improve and be maintained. The "**5 R's**" of Sōsh discussed in this book provide specific strategies to accomplish this goal.

As the child's world expands beyond the family home, their most significant relationships occur with the school, neighborhood, and community. Parents are no longer the ultimate authorities they once were, although they remain very important to the child's overall development. In conjunction with the expansion of how the child sees the world is an increased awareness of the realities of the world. Thus, children now experience real world fears and anxieties that can interfere with social success. For example, a child might not want to go to the school carnival because it is tornado season and there could be a storm.

As the child begins to focus on connecting with other kids from school or his neighborhood, having adults available to facilitate these relationships is of the essence. Because parents cannot be available in schools, and because having parents around is becoming increasingly "embarrassing" for the child this age, school professionals should be responsible for facilitating social relationships during the school day. Further, using peer mentors and supports can be a means of removing the immediate adult facilitator and instead allowing adults to supervise the peer supports from a distance. Peer mediators, coaches, mentors, and "buddies" (these are mostly interchangeable terms depending on the school's approach) are critical to the social progress of a child during this stage. The specific role of these peers will be discussed further in the **Sōsh in Schools** chapter.

Children have stronger and more focused interests during this stage, which is often why individuals with more subtle indications of a neurodevelopmental diagnosis (e.g., Asperger's Syndrome) may not be accurately identified until the "switch" turns on around age 8 or 9 years old. Indeed, most social interactions are initially accomplished and available because the parent or caregiver takes the child to play groups and play dates during the early years and then enrolls the child in early childhood education, which is also play-based. During these stages of development, children focus more on activities than on relationships.

The focus on objects or topics is in sharp contrast to the so-called 'tween years of development that occur between 9 and 12 years of age in which children begin to depend on the peer group more for enjoyment and connection, and interests must be developmentally appropriate or the child risks being rejected. For example, continuing to love Legos in the fifth grade may not provide the same strength of "relationship glue" to keep a child connected with his peers that it did in the second grade. Although there may be a few peers "just like" the child who continue to enjoy playing with Legos, the majority of the peer group is making its developmental shift into relationships based on thoughts about topics such as sports and pop culture versus an interest in toys. Indeed, this is the stage in which functional play is replaced by companionship with others.

Adolescence: 12 - 18 Years

Prior to this stage, according to Erikson, development mostly depends upon what happens to the child. In other words, the child is a passive recipient of development. From this stage forward (ages 12 to 18 years), development depends primarily on what the child (dare I say, young adult) does. This means that the child must now actively work on development on his own and will make gains according to his self-directed efforts. And while adolescence is a stage in which children are transitioning between their childhood and adulthood, life is becoming more complex as children attempt to establish a sense of identity, experience difficulties with social interactions, and debate moral issues.

For successful development to occur, the individual must differentiate (become someone who is separate from the family of origin) and integrate as a "contributing" member of society. Unfortunately for those around the child, as the child navigates this stage he may go into a period of withdrawing from responsibilities, which Erikson called a "moratorium." This is one reason why people often refer to teens as "lazy" or "unmotivated" at one point or another. Further, if an individual is unsuccessful in navigating this stage he will experience role confusion and upheaval (i.e., emotional stress or difficulties due to not having a sense of where he "fits" or belongs in the world). The result can be frequent arguments between parent and teen about motivation, drive, goals, direction of life, and laziness.

A significant task for adolescents is to establish a philosophy of life. In this process, teens tend to think in terms of ideals (i.e., how it *should* be), which are conflict-free, rather than reality (i.e., how it *is*), which is not. The problem (and the reason why adults and teens often argue during this period of development) is that teens do not have much experience and find it easy to substitute ideals for experience. Parents, on the other hand, have experience in the real world and thus tend to put the brakes on the teen's idealistic thinking, which upsets the teen brain. Teens also develop strong devotion to friends and causes. Thus, it should come as no surprise that the teen's most significant relationships are with peer groups, who just so happen also to utilize and value this idealistic style of thinking. This is a period of development in which many teens take on volunteer work or begin to participate in organizations for the "greater good." Erikson believed that if parents allow and encourage the child to explore, he will conclude his own identity. However, if the parents continually push him to conform to their adult views, the teen will face identity confusion which results in not being able to make a successful transition into independent adulthood.

Young Adulthood: 18 - 35 Years

In the initial stage of adulthood most of us seek companions and love. As we try to find mutually satisfying relationships (primarily through dating, marriage, and friendships), we generally also start a family. The age at which one begins family planning is later today with many waiting to start families until their thirties. If negotiating this stage of development is successful, intimacy is experienced on a deep level.

If a person is unsuccessful at finding companionship and love, isolation and distance from others may occur. When it is difficult to create satisfying relationships, the world can shrink and, in defense, Erickson believed that individuals may begin to convince themselves that they are superior to others. Some young adults with social difficulties, who have been unsuccessful in improving their level of functioning, may cite their "superior intellect" or the "boring interests" of the rest of the world as an excuse for why they don't have friends (e.g., "Why would I want to sit down and listen to a bunch of imbeciles talk about sports?"). It is easier to blame everyone else for their difficulties than it is to acknowledge their own limitations.

Erickson identified additional stages through the lifespan, but they are beyond the age range of the Sōsh approach and beyond my area of specialization. The Sōsh approach is ideal for children through young adults in their late 20's and early 30's.

Scaffold According to Development

It is essential to find the ideal time in development in which the child is ready to accomplish something and determine that they have an adequate foundational skill set to do it. The preceding sections of this chapter were written to help you understand what occurs during various stages of a child's development so that you can plan your approach accordingly. Teaching a child a new skill at the opportune point in their development sets him up for positive experiences and positive emotions. It is extremely rewarding when a child makes developmental gains. Parents must remember to challenge the child throughout the process of development in order for the child to continue to make gains. Be aware of the tightrope walk that family members experience. Many families ask me, "How do I know when to push and when I am pushing too hard?" I respond, "When you ask a child to execute a social skill or interaction and he successfully completes it without help, he could already do it. He has learned nothing. You need to raise the stakes. If he is completely overwhelmed, then we need to reevaluate the goals or address whatever may be getting in the way (e.g., anxiety or mood difficulties)." It is important for parents to gradually release responsibility to the child until the social skill can be executed independently, as explained below.

Once the "switch" turns on in the child's brain and he is intrinsically motivated to improve his social skills, the parent is now presented with a critical opportunity to engage with the child and begin to "scaffold" the child's social development. The scaffold (Vygotsky, 1978) is the term used to describe the environment the parent or adult creates, the instructional support, and the processes and language that are used to help improve social skills with the child. Please be aware, however, that this approach can and should be used for younger children as well, even if the "switch" has yet to turn on in their brains. The primary difference is that the younger child may not have as much motivation to acquire new social skills. However, this does not mean that they cannot learn something new. There is a strong focus on early intervention for children with developmental delays (e.g., limited expressive language) because of the significant effect it can have in helping the child make the necessary gains. In terms of social delays, however, I consider ages nine through fourteen to be the "Early Intervention" period given that the child's motivation to make gains in this area does not truly begin until this period of time.

Scaffolding should include what is near to the child's experience or what they can already do well, and build to what is further from their experience, or what they should or need to be able to do. A number of steps are involved to effectively scaffold a child. An adult cannot simply create a scaffold and expect the child to "climb" it on his own. Instead, the adult needs to build the scaffold with the child and **ASSIST** the child by following these steps (Stone, 1993):

- **Arouse** interest in a new social skill or build on a social skill that already captures a child's interest.
- **Simplify** the skill, helping the child complete certain steps or aspects of the skill.
- **Scaffold** the skill so that it is within the child's ability, perhaps by being part of the interaction or arranging the environment so that success is possible.
- **Interpret** the interaction so that the child's cognitive understand and reasoning will facilitate skill mastery.
- **Solve** problems and anticipate mistakes and guide the child to avoid or correct them.
- **Teach** enthusiasm by encouraging the desire to achieve and by keeping the child interested and keeping confidence high by praising success.

Kids can and do develop new social skills and abilities when adults lead them through interactions. Depending on various factors, an adult will lend various levels of assistance over various iterations of the interactions. The goal is to allow the child to do as much as they can on their own, and then to intervene and provide assistance when it is needed so that the task can be successfully completed. This allows the child to learn the particular skill and further their overall social skills development.

An example of ASSIST in everyday practice would be helping a child with a jigsaw puzzle. In order to **Arouse** the interest of the child, the puzzle might need to have a theme of one of his favorite characters (e.g., Thomas the Tank Engine or Toy Story). You would then **Simplify** and **Scaffold** by arranging pieces by type, such as outer edge pieces, and then helping the child find pieces and even doing some hand-over-hand completion. Talking aloud while completing the puzzle helps to **Interpret** and improve the child's cognitive skills (e.g., "This piece has a blue edge so it probably fits in the top part of the puzzle where there is sky"). **Solve** would involve troubleshooting any difficulties along the way such as moving on to find another piece after trying to force a different piece into a section that is clearly the wrong size. Finally, praising the child's persistence and success completing the puzzle helps to build esteem and encourage future interest in the activity (i.e., **Teach**).

Parents and Other Adults as Social Coaches: A "How To" Guide

For parents who remain unsure of how to begin helping a child develop social skills, I advocate using the teaching approach that is utilized by many medical schools: *See One, Do One, Teach One.* The parent or adult first models a new strategy in the appropriate context and has the child watch or "*See One.*" As this is done, the parent describes what the strategy is, when the strategy should be used, and how to go about using it. For example, let's assume the parent chooses a board game as a tool to teach the child turn-taking and problem-solving. The first approach would be to model playing the game with another adult as they describe what they are doing and why they are doing it. The adult might say, "Okay. We are going to pick game pieces first. I will be red. What color would you like to be? The instructions say 'the youngest player starts'. I am older than you, so you get to go first." This example is specific to a younger child and would be adjusted according to the age of the child you are coaching. Depending on the child's profile, the adult may need to repeat the *See One* process numerous times to provide the necessary modeling.

Once the child is ready to move on, the next step on the continuum is for the parent to engage in the task *with* the child. Thus, we now ask the child to "*Do One.*" In the board game example, the child now plays with the adult. The adult looks for opportunities to reinforce appropriate behavior and coach when necessary. Remember to keep feedback statements positive and tell the child what they need to do instead of what not to do. Finally, give the child time to problem solve and generate solutions. Too often, adults ask children what else they could have done, but don't wait long enough for them to answer. By waiting, the child has more time and thus is more likely to generate an appropriate solution. The adult's response, consistent with the approaches of positive feedback and telling the child what to do, should be, "Oh, I love your idea. You came up with a really smart solution. I am especially proud of how you took the time to think that through." When the child is provided with time to generate the solution, he acquires ownership over the idea. When they own the idea, they are more likely to use that strategy again in the future and generalize it to other contexts.

The third step is for the child to take over the task of using the strategy with the parent helping and intervening as needed. This is when it would be ideal for the child to try to play the board game with a peer as well as the parent. The child would be asked to explain the rules and facilitate the play (i.e., *"Teach One"*) with the adult helping out as needed.

Finally, the child independently uses the strategies he has learned while the parent watches. Thus, the children are allowed to play together with the adult present but no longer an active participant in the board game. If a child experiences difficulty using a strategy in a particular situation, the parent may have to move back a step by providing help, or taking over the task and asking the child to help.

Walk the Line

Parents and others working on social difficulties with a child often need a reminder not to push social development too forcefully before the child is interested and motivated. I liken this approach to trying to nail Jell-O to a wall. It's not going to stick and will only frustrate you. Often, when the "switch" in the brain "turns on" (as discussed previously) at around nine years of age, there is a strong desire on behalf of adults to work quickly and thus rush the process. After all, many parents have been waiting a long time for this moment and are excited to start making some serious progress. Not rushing requires patience with the developmental process (working within the pace that the child is currently progressing), relaxation, and the celebration of successes (as small as they may be at times) along the way. Significant gains can be made without unnecessary pressure on the child to "just be social." Knowing that parents are supportive and "along for the ride" as "scaffolds" can be a big boost to the child's confidence and comfort as he embarks on this complicated, yet ultimately rewarding journey.

It is normal, healthy, and important for the child to experience a degree of anxiety and stress along the way, as these serve as motivating factors as well as a barometer to indicate that the child is being challenged. Establishing a meter by which anxiety is measured is vital. For example, consider having the child rate his anxiety on a scale between 1-10 with "1" representing *mild* anxiety and "10" reflecting *profound* anxiety (change the rating qualifiers as needed depending on the age of the child). In the absence of this the child may become overly stressed and debilitated to the point that any desire to practice these interactions and skills stops. Indeed, continuing to push a child who consistently reports an anxiety rating of "10" will result in failure to accomplish goals. The approach you use is only as good as the timing, guidance, and support system that accompany it. Consult with a third party such as a child psychologist to offer a neutral, yet professional, perspective on the degree that you are pushing the child and also analyze how much the child can tolerate during that particular stage in time. Setting goals with the child is a good way of agreeing in advance on what will be worked on and can help the child feel involved in his social development. All of these tools and strategies will be explained in detail as you read through this book.

Key Points

- Understanding child development theory is essential to helping a child with social skills difficulty.

- Piaget and Erickson provide two essential theories to guide social skills development.

- A child's chronological or birth age is not always consistent with a child's developmental age. Understanding a child's level of development and targeting a social skills approach based on that level, and not the child's age, is essential.

- Play is important to ALL ages. Younger children learn best with physical play and hands-on learning. As children grow, they interpret the world through pretend play with objects, and finally play is associated with ideas. Parents should always encourage play. The approach is simple: Put in the time and have fun!

- The first relationships of importance to children are with parents and close family. Parents become less influential as a child develops, although parents always remain an integral part of a child's development.

- As a child grows, his relationships become more intimate and focused on interpersonal values rather than objects.

- Exposure to a variety of peers and environments outside of the child's comfort zone of home and siblings (or relatives) is essential.

- Children experience a phenomenon that I have coined the "switch" of social development on or around their ninth birthday regardless of their development in other areas. This is the time in which children begin to experience their own motivation to connect with others socially, whereas adults were the ones encouraging these interactions prior to this time. I consider ages nine through fifteen to be the "Early Intervention" period for social skills.

- Parents and other adults can scaffold a child's social development by following a progressive approach that involves modeling and explaining, interacting with the child alone, interacting with the child and a peer together, observing a child and the peer, and then allowing the child to play with a peer alone.

- Parents must "Walk the Line," which involves supporting the child while also challenging him to participate in new social opportunities.

- In order to "scaffold" a child's social progress we must ASSIST him. This involves **Arousing** interest in learning the skill, **Simplifying** what we ask him to do, **Scaffold** or support the child completing the skill so success is possible, **Interpret** the interaction so that the child's cognitive understand and reasoning will facilitate skill mastery, **Solve** problems with the child as they arise, and **Teach** enthusiasm by keeping the child interested and keeping confidence high by praising success.

- *See One, Do One, Teach One* allows the child to see how the skill should be used, practice doing the skill with some support, and show/teach the skill to someone younger or less experienced to solidify mastery.

Chapter Three

Relate: Connect with Others

Relate: Connect with Others

Sarah, a 10-year-old girl, walked into my office and immediately began to pretend that she was a mythical creature. Her love for fantasy was quickly apparent and, as if to further illustrate this, she wore a t-shirt with the picture of a unicorn on the front. Her parents report that her peers are noticing that she is "different" with regard to her social interactions. Indeed, Sarah prefers, if not insists, that others focus on topics that she is comfortable discussing (e.g., Pokemon, Nintendo, medieval history). Her language is often "scripted" in nature and her parents question whether they are talking to Sarah or a cartoon character that she is mimicking. Her nonverbal gestures are caricatures of actors or cartoon figures from television or popular culture. She speaks to imaginary friends and engages in pretend play privately because she is concerned that her parents "will think it's weird."

Sarah talks loudly and has difficulty modulating her voice volume, rate, and tone. Her mother reports that she rarely cried when she was younger, but now she easily becomes upset over seemingly trivial events. Behaviorally, she is not aggressive but instead bottles things up. New and unfamiliar situations are stressful for her. Sarah would prefer to know in advance all of the details of her day so that she can anticipate situations.

Sarah is able to engage with others, provided they play with her the way she dictates. Sarah is essentially unaware of the feelings or thoughts of others. Thus, she is currently experiencing social difficulties due to her expectation that her peers should have the same interests.

I really enjoyed working with Sarah. However, I also understood how her peer group may be frustrated with her because of her need to control play and the unusual content of her play (e.g., medieval themes). In the **Introduction** chapter of this book, the importance of practicing social interactions in the moment was discussed. The first of the "**5R's**" of the Sōsh approach is **Relate** (Connect with Others). The purpose of **Relate** is to guide children, families, and teachers through a number of effective strategies and approaches to help with a child's social development. To many, the ability to connect with others is the most important or certainly most identifiable area of social skills difficulties. The child's difficulty connecting with others inhibits him from improving his skills in all areas of development and eventually affects mood, behavior, and even school performance. This chapter contains the strategies necessary to help a child begin to connect with others.

Out and About

To experiment with the social world, people must be *out and about*. In other words, they have to go to social settings and interact. This is obviously difficult for kids who struggle socially. Therefore, this approach needs to be framed less about the event itself (e.g., play date, football game, after school activity) and more about the opportunity to be with people. Using a football game as an example, a child can attend the game and even just stand on, or next to, the bleachers with other kids cheering. This alone can be helpful. Perhaps the child can strike up a conversation with someone nearby or comment about something that happened on the field. He may not become friends with this person; indeed, the child may not have anything in common with this person, but he has now practiced social skills by making small talk--and that is an accomplishment. If the child is not comfortable socializing directly with others, then maybe he could volunteer to sell parking passes, take tickets, work as the team manager, help in the concessions stand, or dress as the team's mascot. There are numerous "jobs" that can help create opportunities for social interactions without the pressure of spontaneous interaction. All of these activities allow for practice of basic social skills (e.g., making eye contact while taking a ticket).

If the individual has sensory issues, he can still be in the stadium but seated away from the louder sections. A common treatment approach for auditory sensitivity is to desensitize the aversion to loud noises by gradual exposure to these noises over time. Sensory buffers such as earplugs (or even using a set of iPod headphones) can be useful. The idea is to use these headphones initially to involve the child in the activity and then encourage them to take the headphones off when he begins to feel more comfortable in the environment. Eventually, the child may not need them at all when entering the situation. As with most of the approaches in this book, it is important to walk the line between challenging the child and enabling them. The goal is to ensure that the child is comfortable enough to make progress, but also uncomfortable enough to make progress.

Behavior Before Mood

A necessary social approach, provided that the child is not experiencing a clinically significant level of depression, is to coach the principle of the behavior occurring before the mood. An individual may not feel, for example, that they would *like* to go to a high school football game on Friday night, attend the Homecoming dance, or go to the birthday party, but going to the football game, dance, or birthday party may actually end up being tolerable if not fun.

The behavior must come *before* the desired feeling. Specifically, individuals must attend the football game, even if it is uncomfortable, before they can experience the feelings of improved self-esteem or confidence, for example. Most children, although they object to this initially, will report that once they were at the event it was not so bad, and they actually enjoyed themselves. If a child is depressed, then a consultation with a mental health professional may be necessary to determine the child's current ability to put their behavior before their mood. In any other cases, though, a person is *able* to put the behavior before the mood, although they may not *want* to.

When implementing this exercise, keep the expectations reasonable. Just attend an event. **That's it, plain and simple: attend the event**. Get out of the house for an hour and then you can come back home. Remind the child that he is already able to do this each day when he attends school. When beginning this approach, it doesn't matter if the child talks to anyone. It doesn't matter if the child makes eye contact with anyone. There is plenty of time to work on these "skills." One of the biggest hurdles may be convincing the child to leave their home because they often do not "feel" like it. This is the time that we must remember that the behavior must come before the mood. Some families even schedule mandatory outings to accomplish this goal, such as going to the library every Wednesday evening from 5 p.m. to 6 p.m. to complete homework.

Children regularly return to my office and tell me that, although they were very upset with me and did not want to go to the specific event (e.g., school dance, Boy Scouts meeting, football game), they took a risk and it went okay. Although they felt "awful" prior to attending the event, once they were there they realized it wasn't so bad. It certainly was not as bad as they predicted. Further, the strategy of simply being *in* the social environment paid off because there was no pressure to achieve any outcome other than attendance initially, so any interactions that occurred spontaneously were a bonus.

I generally recommend that a child participate in at least one structured activity away from the home each week. Preschool, kindergarten, and elementary school do not count toward this time. For younger children who are not yet attending school, these activities are often chosen by the parent and may include: play dates, Kindermusik, toddler gymnastics, dance classes, or library story times. School-aged children have more access to after-school clubs like chess, robotics, dramatic arts, or debate. Volunteer positions, community service, or even a part-time job meet this requirement for teens and young adults.

Managing Stress

When trying to help younger children who may feel anxious in social situations, it can be more effective to focus on the specific task rather than the overall social picture. For example, telling the child, "We're going over to Billy's house for an hour to play Candyland and have a snack" will be met with much less anxiety than, "We're going over to Billy's for a play date." The first directive is measurable and predictable. The child now knows explicitly what to expect, which helps to reduce stress and anxiety. The child also has a sense of when the play date will end. Indeed, once the hour is over we will go back to the car and drive home, end of story. However, with the open-ended play date scenario, what will take place and for how long are much less clear. Thus, the child may experience an increase in anxiety. Children like Sarah, who we met at the beginning of the chapter, can become anxious not knowing what to expect, which then causes some children to act out behaviorally, making it difficult to even get out of the house.

To help the child, prepare him for how long the visit will last, what will happen, and where it will take place (e.g., "We are going to Jill's house for an hour to play three games and have a snack"). If time is a confusing concept or not yet understood, use the completion of activities to signify when the play date will end (e.g., "We will play three games and then leave") or use a timer to show a countdown of the time remaining.

If you are going to meet on a playground, for example, try to focus the child's attention on the familiar elements of that setting to decrease the stress related to the play date. It will be easier for the younger child to focus on what playground equipment he will play on rather than what he will say or do with his play partner. Also, a familiar playground setting allows the child to anticipate the setting from memory, which always helps to alleviate anxiety. This is true with social events for older children as well (e.g., dance class, karate). Providing the child with concrete information (e.g., "Dance class lasts for one hour and you will practice ballet") will ease their anxiety.

The success of the strategies presented throughout this **Relate** chapter is dependant on the "Okay, now what?" principle that must be utilized by parents. Even the most well-intentioned and prepared parents must ask themselves this question each step of the way. In the playground example, the child has been prepared for the play visit at that location and has some activities that he is looking forward to once he arrives (e.g., he will swing and then go down the slide). However, the "Okay, now what?" moment arrives when the focus naturally shifts from the activity to the people who will also be there. While it is important for the child (and parent) to be "brave" and follow through with putting the behavior before mood, it is equally important to coach the child, initially, as they begin to interact more with other kids in the environment. So, how do you coach and ultimately facilitate the development of the peer relationship once you are out and about? You should first learn and review the ASSIST and *See One, Do One, Teach One* strategies described in the **Development** chapter before proceeding with the following strategies.

Facilitating Interactions: Young Child

When trying to remediate social skills difficulties with a child, remember that he may be functioning a few years (or more in some instances) behind his chronological age with regard to his social abilities. Thus, you may have a 6-year-old child who responds to and interacts socially with the world much as a 4-year-old would. This gap is often difficult for society, and some parents, to comprehend or accept. When a 30-year-old man has the social skills of a 28-year-old, there is rarely any cause for alarm. In fact, most wives expect at least this much of a maturity gap in their husbands! However, the kindergarten student who acts, developmentally, like a 3-year-old is much more apparent.

It is essential to avoid comparing your child's progress with that of his same-age peers. Try to remain flexible with your expectations rather than think, "He's old enough and *should* be doing this on his own by now." What I say to parents is, based on his age, he *should* be doing lots of things socially by now, but he's not. There are certainly feelings of anger, frustration, and sadness that accompany this realization. However, continually pointing out your frustration and his delay doesn't help the situation. In order to achieve social gains, the approach taken with children should be practical and realistic, and thus based on the child's current level of development.

Parents and caregivers must act as coaches, teachers, and therapists for the child with social skills difficulties. What other children may be able to accomplish in the social domain with relative ease as a result of typical development may require explicit instruction for their socially delayed peer counterparts. This instruction can begin at home with parents and siblings as play partners, but it *must* eventually transition outside of the home (e.g., school, extracurricular activities, neighborhood gatherings) to include the peer group.

One reason I stress the importance of getting out and interacting with various peers is that the immediate family will always be a source of comfort and security for the child. Thus, performance is always at its best around those with whom the child is most familiar. This is initially a good thing, especially if the child feels anxious about interacting with unfamiliar kids. However, most of us want our children to go to school, make friends, graduate high school, go to college, get a job, and perhaps even settle down in a long-term relationship. To accomplish these goals, children need to begin at the most comfortable level that allows them to create a sound social foundation. It is essential, though, that the necessary exploration occurs and that comfort does not become debilitating. There is a "dance" of allowing a certain degree of comfort and relaxation while pushing for change, which is inherently uncomfortable. Remember from the **Development** chapter that the primary social unit for children seven years and younger is the family. However, when your child is school-age, the peer group must become an integral part of the child's social interactions.

The best way to facilitate social interactions with younger kids (typically 18 months through kindergarten), is: 1) Provide opportunities for the child to meet up with a play mate ("buddy" or "peer" for the older child, although the terms are synonymous), and 2) Be in the moment (at least initially) with the child as he attempts to navigate the situation and the relationship. The "in the moment" person should be the parent before the child is in school, and should help model and intervene using the *See One*, *Do One*, *Teach One* and ASSIST methods described in the **Development** chapter.

At the younger stages and ages of development the parents possess more motivation for the child to succeed socially. To reiterate, social functioning is enhanced and improved with exposure to social opportunities and in-the-moment guidance from parents during those interactions. If you don't believe this, try talking to your preschooler, while you drive him to a play group, about how you expect him to behave and then setting him loose in a room of toys and kids and see how much of that mini-lecture is retained. Instead, the child may take a toy from another child, for example, and you walk (or run!) over to him and troubleshoot accordingly. You may have to replay this intervention several or even dozens of times before learning takes effect, but you never give up on the child's ability to learn and thus you continue teaching. Children from birth through kindergarten age learn by *doing*, not by listening.

Just because parents begin (and need) to involve others in their child's development as they grow older does not mean that parents stop teaching. This lifelong need for teaching reminds me of some dialogue from one of my favorite movies, *Parenthood*. Steve Martin's character, Gill, is talking to his father, played by Jason Robards. Gill's father explains the longevity of parenting this way: "There's no goal line in parenting, no end zone where you spike the ball, do your touchdown dance and that's it. Whether [the child is] 25 or 45 or 65. It never ends. Never." Thus, parents always remain involved, but must learn when to step up and when to back off, depending on the child's progress through development. I often refer to this as the "Kenny Rogers school of parenting": *Know when to hold 'em and know when to fold 'em.* It is much easier to facilitate play between two 3-year-olds than between two 9-year-olds or even two teenagers. Three-year-olds allow their parents to be more involved in their play and pay attention to feedback (provided it is given effectively). With older children, coaching must come in a well-timed comment in passing or while driving on an errand or even right before bed at night when reflecting on your day together. Parents typically have to be more creative in their teaching tactics as children grow older.

When implementing social skills strategies, it is important to remember that it will be difficult for the child to accept any new approach. The very idea that the child requires an "approach" to social skills underscores a deficit, which immediately sets off warning bells and puts him off. Therefore, a key component to success is increasing the amount of positive feedback given. Every social attempt should be reinforced. Just think of how many opportunities exist to engage socially each day, especially if the child enjoys going out to various places. For example, imagine that your child walks into the middle of a group of kids playing with trading cards, interrupts and says, "My favorite cartoon is

Spongebob." Instead of pulling the child aside and telling him how inappropriate his behavior or comment was, your feedback should start off with a positive statement. For example, "I'm glad you wanted to share something about yourself with those kids." Then a corrective statement can be made: "I noticed they were playing with cards and were not talking about cartoons. I wonder what you could have done differently to join their game?" In this manner, the child learns that he did something right in the interaction (i.e., he initiated an interaction with the others) which helps build his self-esteem, but it also creates a teaching moment and an opportunity to problem solve. With that approach in mind, let's consider who we can practice these skills with and when we should do so.

Who is the Ideal Play Partner for a Young Child?

The decision of *who* to have a child interact with plays a role in the overall social development of the child. This choice of play partner and the context of the play are equally important to help a child with social skills difficulties. For example, having the child play primarily with siblings or other relatives (e.g., cousins) certainly helps to establish foundational skills at a younger age (e.g., the toddler years), but ultimately familiarity reigns supreme and the quality of these interactions is not as dynamic as it would be with non-family members or unfamiliar individuals such as an unrelated play partner. Thus, parents must give thoughtful consideration to who the child will play with prior to the point in which the child can make those decisions for himself. It is typically appropriate to help select play mates prior to the child's entry into first grade. If you are like most parents, you will want to take advantage of this rare time in a child's development in which you have almost exclusive say over who they interact with. It will only be a matter of time (hint: teen years) when this selection of peers becomes a point of contention.

I frequently give parents a "play date assignment" to help in this endeavor. The goal is to schedule play dates with non-family members as often as possible, in 1:1 ratios and in groups (ranging from small to larger, structured play groups). Parents often struggle with this assignment and are plagued with questions: How old should the play partner be? What should the skill set of the play partner be? How long should the play visit last? What should occur during the play visit? Where do I find a play partner for the child?

Regarding the age of the play partner, older children are more proficient play partners but the general guideline is to locate a play partner who is approximately the same age or in the same grade as the child. In terms of skill sets, the partner must be a child who can model appropriate social interactions and be patient with the child who requires some assistance, while not doing all of the work. This is where parents and other adults serve a crucial role as they mediate these interactions, helping the children strike a balance between giving and receiving help, for example.

The phrase "birds of a feather flock together" comes to mind when considering who we select as our peer group. When training to run in a race, coaches often recommend finding a running partner who is slightly faster so that you will work harder to keep up. The same principle applies to children with social skills difficulties. The child should always have appropriate peer models so that social skills can be modeled upward. Kids will work harder to "match" the peer model's skills and keep up. Further, the greater the variety of peers that the child is exposed to, in as many situations as possible, the broader the child's social adaptability.

Play visits should alternate between the homes of the children involved and neutral locations such as playgrounds, libraries, or other kid-friendly locales. Neutral locations allow more spontaneous and flexible interactions to occur such as another, perhaps unfamiliar, child joining play. The length of the visit is often dependent on a variety of factors including the activity and the age/attentional capacity of the kids. A good starting point is to keep it time-limited to about one hour, allowing flexibility to play longer if things go well. My recommendation is to quit while you are ahead and still having fun and end the play visit on a positive note. No parent wants to end a play date with a tantrum because the children are tired or frustrated. Ending the visit while everyone is happy helps to promote excitement and interest in a future play meeting.

What should occur during play visits is also dependent on the child's developmental level, age, abilities, and interests. A general principle is to begin with structured activities (e.g., board games, physical play such as *Hide and Seek*, a snack). As kids demonstrate fluency in interactions, the adult involvement can decrease as the kids' involvement increases. Remember that social skills are not improving if the kids are watching a TV show together or doing any other activity that is not interactive. Further, allowing one child to play with Legos on one side of a room while the other child plays across the room is not interactive either. Although the entire session does not have to be interactive, and breaks are okay, it is important to encourage as much interaction as possible, especially during time-limited play opportunities.

The answer to the question of *where* to find a play partner for your child can be tricky. Depending on where you live, you may have more options. Families that live in rural areas, for example, may be limited in terms of their built-in neighborhood network of kids. This is why the Sōsh *Out and About* approach is encouraged. The more opportunities you have to be out and around other people, the greater your chances of meeting various kids who could be possible play partners, as recommended by the research regarding social skills improvement (White et al., 2007). Good places to find other parents and kids include the library (they usually offer a storytime activity for kids), reading time at local bookstores, community classes, dance, karate, church, local parks, and clubs (e.g., Boy Scouts). Many play dates develop out of play groups with several mothers who connect. Creativity and an open mind are essential here. If one play partner does not work out, keep trying. As you work through the strategies outlined in this book, you increase the chances of repeat play dates. If truly at a loss for where to find play partners, consider looking for postings on the internet such as Meetup.com or even create your own *Yahoo!* Group or similar website to begin establishing play dates. These sites allow people to meet in public locations as a group so that all parties involved are safe and comfortable. Individual play dates can then be established based on the participants' individual levels of comfort with each other.

Facilitating Interactions: Older Child

If you recall from the **Development** chapter, a child's brain flips a "switch" around his ninth year of life in which he begins to desire social connections with peers. While this is an exciting time, many kids lack the skills to achieve these connections. This presents quite a Catch-22 for parents as well as their children. One way to solve this is to help the child search outside of the immediate family unit for friends. When the child has this natural instinct to establish friendships, parents must move away from telling the child who their "friends" are and instead nurture and support the child's desire to connect with peers on their own terms. One thing that can be done, as we allow the child more control and freedom over their selection of "friends," is to steer the child in the right direction.

This will require more advice, suggestion, and guidance and may result in debates. The point is to give the child a sense of control over the process while still serving as a guidance counselor from a safe distance.

I recommend parents help facilitate this process initially by encouraging the child to connect with *one* person. Once the "switch" in the child's brain is flipped, make sure to keep expectations low initially. Start out slow and simple. Parents must prepare themselves to feel some (or a lot) of anxiety as they begin this process. This anxiety is normal and can be more pronounced depending on the level of social difficulty that the child has. It's best, when trying to help an older child connect, to begin by conducting a strategic planning session to determine who might be an ideal candidate to connect with initially.

Friends Venn Diagram

Many of the kids I work with are visual learners, so a visual representation is useful to identify possible candidates for friendship or "peer companionship." Start simple with a goal to approach one person who the child wants to get to know (e.g., from school or from the neighborhood). The way I demonstrate this is to draw two concentric circles on a piece of paper so the circles overlap in the middle and I then write the name of the person the child is interested in connecting with in one circle, and the child's name that I am working with in the remaining circle.

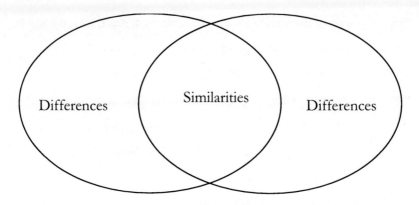

The child is asked to identify the differences between what *he* likes and what the *other* person likes. Then, the child identifies what similarities exist and enters those in the center area. The adult can then coach the child about the need for common ground to facilitate a connection with the other person. For example, let's say the child plays violin but his peer plays piano. He insists that they have nothing in common because they play *different* instruments. We use this diagram to illustrate that although the instruments are different, both children play music which is the similarity. This exercise helps kids identify that they can connect with others even though they may have differences. Once the individual is comfortable making connections based on similarities, they can move onto other challenges. He might hear someone talk about something, for example, that he disagrees with or knows little about, but he could return the conversation to a topic of shared interest. If daring, he might even try to learn about a new interest or topic despite it not being consistent with something he enjoys!

The goal, again, is to help the child find at least *one* person he can connect with. One person might not initially seem like a big accomplishment, but it is a big difference from zero. Once the child has one connection, they can develop the skills to lead them to two and three friends. If the child is very anxious about making a connection, it may be helpful to build confidence in a non-threatening environment. Some strategies to assist with confidence building are discussed in the next section.

Let's Get a Pizza

In the context of my social skills groups and individual counseling work, I try to find as many opportunities as possible to take kids "into the field," such as the shopping mall that is across from my office building. No one in the mall knows that we are in the middle of a therapy session as we walk casually together through the mall, and, for the older child, being in the mall with me is not as embarrassing as being with mom or dad. I first model the behaviors we have worked on to ease the child's anxiety before asking them to take a turn and practice the skills(s).

Generally, the task for the child is to walk up to individuals who are employed in various stores and generate questions regarding the retail business such as, "Do you have any [item you are looking for] in stock?" or, "Where can I find the latest [fill in your favorite movie] DVD?" This could be done from home if the child prefers to practice asking questions over the telephone initially, although using the face-to-face approach is ideal. For some children with social skills difficulties, interacting with adults is fairly easy and comfortable so it works well as a first step. As they complete this task, increasing the difficulty is essential to ensure progress. The child can talk with younger store clerks, or approach kids who are also shopping, to ask them something such as the time or where a store is located.

Another idea related to phone calls involves pizza night, which is a staple in many families. In this case, why not let the child practice their social skills by calling and ordering the pizza? Making a phone call still requires the child to work through some anxiety, and the phone is a useful starting tool for kids who are anxious because it does not require facing the person on the other end of the line. This person does not know who they are speaking with, and the child is unlikely to ever run into this person or see this person in their lifetime (some kids respond quite well to such a dramatic generalization).

As an aside, the food order exercise must be completed during times you actually need something to eat. I have worked with kids who like to practice ordering pizzas they don't plan to eat (or pay for) and the pizza company ends up calling me to complain after the child so honestly informed the manager that it was his therapist's idea!

If the child wants additional practice, they are encouraged to call stores so they can ask questions. The child can call a department store and ask for the electronics department, for example. Think of an item and find out if they have it available, or call the store to get directions or find out what their operating hours are. Even if the store provides all of this information in the automated greeting, wait to speak with someone or press "0" to speak with a customer associate and ask them anyway. It doesn't matter if the child needs the information or not, practicing will increase conversational comfort. It also helps to generate small talk. The child is simply establishing a temporary connection with another person, and in the process, developing a skill set that will be valuable in the long run. There is almost guaranteed success with this exercise provided the child will do it.

In the event the child refuses to complete this exercise or is uncomfortable (as many kids often are in the beginning), then the parent can model a phone call or two and then have the child attempt a phone call with some support. One strategy is to turn on the speaker phone and quietly coach the child on what to say based on what the sales associate is saying. Even writing out some questions ahead of time and allowing the child to "script" the approach until comfort sets in is helpful. If your child is truly hesitant then you may need to utilize a reward system for every question that they ask. For example, for every 10-15 seconds they stay on the phone talking to a sales associate (that does not include hold time), they are allowed to stay up ten minutes later in the evening.

Specific Social Skills

Specific social skills such as greeting others or making eye contact are important to improve upon and require some assistance and direct teaching. However, for each of these observable behavioral skills, we see significant difficulties regarding generalizability. The reason for this is that these skills need to be taught and practiced, as much as possible, in natural settings (e.g., home, school, daily outings), rather than in an artificial setting such as a therapist's office.

Most social skills groups that I see advertised deal with specific social skills, which include how to greet people, how to shake hands, how to make eye contact, and how to join a group discussion. These skills are important, especially for parents. These are "comfortable" areas that parents can first report their child is having difficulty with and are willing to acknowledge. Older children will even say to parents, "How do you go up to a group of people standing in the hallway and talk to them?" Indeed, these specific skills groups serve as a first step in the process of admitting or acknowledging, "I want more friends, but I have a hard time making friends." However, kids need to take the specific skills they learn in clinic-based groups and apply them in school and various other social settings as "homework" assignments. Often without practice and support these skills are forgotten and they begin to atrophy like a muscle that has not been exercised. Strategies for the child to practice in his daily environments are outlined in the next section.

Talking Strategies

What Did That Mean?

Two primary aspects of social functioning are: 1) the ability to perceive what others say and do accurately, and 2) the ability to respond appropriately. In order to function well from a social perspective, an individual needs to understand the signals that others are sending and send appropriate signals back to the person.

It is essential for those working with kids with social difficulties to remember that the foundation of communication is nonverbal. Some even argue that language is 93% nonverbal (Mehrabian, 1981). Indeed, something very dramatic happens prior to a child beginning to speak. People have back-and-forth nonverbal communication through facial expressions, like smiling, that occur within the context of play. Parents often focus these early interaction efforts with infants trying to achieve eye contact or to get the child to turn when his name is called. A good example of social referencing is when we say "look," or we shake a rattle in the child's presence and he becomes excited and references the toy. He might then look at us again to share enjoyment before returning his focus back onto the toy. This is a typical developmental benchmark that creates a foundation for social fluency (and language development) in the future.

Even children as young as toddlers can understand basic cues, especially from their parents. They may ask, "Daddy, are you mad?" from their car seat as they overhear dad sigh while stuck in traffic. They are trying to link that particular utterance and behavior to a feeling or emotion, and store it in their memory bank to access later, applying it to new situations and people. This is the beginning of an emotional filing system being created in the brain. Once this experience is stored in the memory, when a similar experience or emotion is observed by the child he will be able to access that "file." Older children can understand nonverbal cues with even more ease. For example, an adolescent may know not to ask for a later curfew right after dad returns home from a bad day at work. Dad may not talk about his bad day at work, but judging from the observable clues such as his hair looking disheveled, his tie loosened, and his brow tightened, the teenager is able to put the pieces together. The timing is not ideal for a later curfew request.

An issue for children with social difficulties is that while they do observe these cues, they tend to interpret them in isolation. They cannot combine them successfully to form a coherent whole. Using the above example of dad coming home stressed, the interpretation of the overall behavioral profile is not one of stress and frustration, but is instead one of isolated behaviors that in and of themselves do not signify the need for the child to modify his behavior. Further, the child does not file this information for later retrieval because each behavior is seen as an isolated incident in time, and thus generalizing these cues and their meanings to similar situations in the future is difficult.

Expressive language, too, can be confusing, especially for children who struggle socially. They may focus on the literal meaning of the words being spoken and less on the nonverbal messages that accompany the expressive language. Complicating this issue, the English language is full of metaphor, idioms, colloquialisms, and figures of speech. The various levels of inflection that speakers use while communicating are incredibly complex. We not only need to listen to the content of what's being spoken when we are having a conversation, but we also must try to infer the meaning behind what it is they are trying to say. Over time, as expressive language develops, children can get their needs met simply by saying, "I want a toy." Adults tend to comply and hand it over. With neurotypical development, which refers to development that occurs on time or as expected, all of the nonverbal aspects will be easily interpreted. But what if you happen to be the child, or the parent of a child, who is not able to pick up on these cues? For example, a child who is told to "get lost" by his peer group may respond by remaining still and looking quizzically at the group. Or a child who is instructed by his coach to cheer on his teammates, but cheers very loudly and at the wrong times, annoying them instead. After all, he was doing what the coach asked by cheering for his teammates, correct?

Children who do not naturally understand the meanings behind idioms and figures of speech and who struggle with nonverbal communication require explicit coaching and encouragement to file this information away for later use. An external storage device or filing method *in addition to* the child's memory might be necessary so that the child can have easy access to this information. The Sōsh mobile app has an *Archive* feature that the person can use to create this filing system. As the person monitors their environment and gathers information of social interactions and their corresponding nonverbal cues, he then "archives" or saves this information in the app for review at a later date. Having this information stored in the device allows accessibility whenever and wherever the person needs it. By frequent review, just like studying material to memorize something, this information can gradually be committed to long-term memory.

Regarding the child's literal interpretations of figures of speech or idioms, looking up the definitions of idioms using the Sōsh app's *What*

Did That Mean? feature can help enhance understanding. The content for this portion of the mobile app was provided by UsingEnglish.com and can also be accessed on their website. The Sōsh app feature allows the child to access this information in the moment and without the peer group's awareness of what they are doing.

Conversation Skills

The previous section focused on the nonverbal signals that accompany the verbal or linguistic code of what is said during conversations. This section addresses how to begin and sustain conversations, but also stresses the importance of *how* words are spoken. Being able to understand and interpret all communication signals accurately is a difficult but necessary skill to engage in fluent conversations.

An important conversational variable to begin practicing, which many speech therapists are skilled at coaching, is conversational pragmatics or the back-and-forth reciprocity of conversation. It is of the utmost importance that children practice taking turns and that parents, teachers, and other supporters of the child monitor his conversations to ensure that he is not dominating the conversation. One of the exercises I often do in my social groups is to tally the amount of questions versus comments made by group members. I developed this idea a number of years ago when I was leading a social group with some preadolescents. It was going along well (I thought) and I was satisfied because, after all, we were having a discussion and all members were participating. However, as I took a step back in order to analyze what was happening, I tuned in to the quality of the conversation and dialogue. I had been focused on the *content* of what the group members were saying, but as I began to listen to the *process*, I noticed that each group member was individually making comments in a collective parallel process. For example, there was a lack of interactive questions such as, "Hey what about this?" or "Why did you like that?" or "Have you seen this?" There was no real attempt to engage in a dialogue. These six children were taking turns making isolated statements about something they each viewed as important. On a surface level, it seemed as if all were participating and by all appearances it was a discussion. The group members seemed satisfied. After all, they were all talking and each had a chance to discuss a topic of their interest which only added to their sense of comfort.

I began to tally the amount of questions versus comments and I limited my measurement to a 10-minute sample of time. Over the course of 10 minutes, there were approximately 90 comments and 2 questions, a lopsided finding to say the least. It is a social skills group phenomenon that can go unnoticed unless you are really tuned into it. In everyday life, this phenomenon can also go unnoticed, but over time other kids (who are able to give and take in their conversations) will say, "Hey, I want a turn. Quit talking!" or will simply avoid talking to the person altogether.

This feedback is useful, even if delivered harshly. Frustrated peers might even say, "Shut up! All you do is talk about the same thing. I don't want to hear about it anymore!" However, the child with social difficulties may simply conclude that the peer is "mean" or may avoid that person so as not to receive any additional negative feedback. Despite the poor delivery of the feedback, this peer is actually doing the child a favor by highlighting this pattern. We can always work with the peer in the future on kinder ways to get the same point across. Boys, especially though, talk to each other this way, so if you hear your child tell you, "Johnny was mean," be sure to get all the information before becoming upset. Johnny could have been doing your child a favor by giving him some needed feedback. It is important to know how others view our children. This provides useful data for treatment planning.

This inevitable "negative" peer feedback is often why children with social skills difficulties seek out younger peers. Younger children don't have strong opinions on the importance of give and take in discussions. The younger child will listen and think it's cool that an older kid is talking to him. The alternative is that the child who is struggling to maintain balance in conversations will seek out adults who will listen and nod their head. Many adults think it is charming and amusing that a child knows so much about European history, for example, and adults are more tolerant of a child who talks incessantly because he is "just a kid" and does not know any better. Unfortunately, both options leave the child at a loss for relationships with same age peers, which is the goal given the amount of time spent at school. In order to increase the potential for the child to initiate and maintain conversations, he needs to be with kids the same age whenever possible. Additional considerations for successful conversations are included below. All of these strategies and skills can be practiced with the help of the Sōsh mobile app.

Eye Contact

One of my favorite ways of practicing eye contact is using technologies such as iPad 2, iPod Touch, and iPhone. Newer versions of these devices include a front facing camera so you can hold the device up and see a reflection of yourself on the screen. You can then record yourself or use it to watch yourself live. The Sōsh application allows for and encourages this exercise in the Eye Contact exercise of the *Talking Strategies* category.

To do this, look directly into your own eyes as you talk. Practicing this repeatedly will help exercise that "muscle" in your brain, making it more habitual. It can be very difficult to practice this with others initially because it requires many skills: looking at the person, listening to what they are saying, thinking about what you are going to say next, and taking a turn to speak at the next available chance. All of these skills must happen smoothly and in this sequence to be successful. It takes a lot of practice to become well-versed in this area of conversational fluency. Just as it takes a lot of time for piano students to learn to use their left hand to play root notes (while reading the bass clef sheet music) while the right hand plays chords or notes (while reading the treble clef sheet music). The music sounds awful when you are first learning and is quite choppy. That's why we practice privately, and often before the big recital.

Body Language & Nonverbals

If a child is experiencing difficulty identifying subtle aspects of conversations such as nonverbals, then he would benefit from focusing the necessary senses. The way to do this is to block out the auditory senses that focus on *what* is being said. Practice this by muting the volume on the video of a conversation while reviewing it. This forces the visual senses to watch for behaviors, mannerisms, and nonverbal cues. When the child is practicing appropriate body language and nonverbal skills in the moment, he should try the following (a parent can help by reading these strategies to the child before or during practice):

1. Face the person. Smile when appropriate. Nod your head up and down if you agree with the person.
2. Consider breaking interactions down into manageable steps. For example, when meeting someone new:

    a.   Choose the correct time to meet the other person.

    b.   Walk up to the person.

    c.   Say your name.

    d.   Wait for the person to tell you his name.

           Ask for the person's name if he does not tell you.

    e.   Shake the person's hand.

    f.   Tell the person something about yourself.

- Ask someone to record video or take a picture of you while you are talking to someone so that you can see how you talk to others. Practice these steps toward a successful conversation:

    1.   Show interest.

    2.   Choose when to talk.

    3.   Start talking in a friendly way.

    4.   Stay on the topic.

    5.   Listen to what the other person says.

    6.   Ask questions.

Speech Rate

- Keep track of the rate of your speech and try to find a balance between talking too fast and too slow. Use audio recording to listen to how you sound.

Speech Volume

- Use the *Regulate >Voice Meter* feature of the Sōsh app to measure the volume of your speech in real time or make an audio recording to hear how loud you speak in conversation.
- One strategy is to slow down your speech if you tend to speak too loudly. This will naturally lower your volume.

Physical Space

- The physical distance between people having a conversation is typically an "arm's length."
- Do not hug others unless you know them well or have asked permission first.
- Ask someone to record video or take a picture of you while you are talking to someone so that you can see how close you are standing.

Turn Taking

- Listen as much as you talk.
- Audio or video record some of your daily conversations and then listen to see how well you take turns in conversation. The *Regulate > Tracking* feature of the Sōsh app can assist with this by allowing the person to tally each instance of pausing for the other person to speak, for example, and then Archiving this tally for later review or sharing with parents or a therapist.

Questions versus Comments

Reminding kids to be an active listener during conversations is essential. This helps alleviate performance anxiety associated with "needing" to keep the dialogue going and is also an important skill. It's okay to listen and ask questions when at a loss for what to say or if you are not fluent in a particular topic. After all, none of us are knowledgeable on every topic. Many of us experience this whether or not we have social difficulties. We may attend a cocktail party and enter into a conversation with someone discussing his occupation, of which we have no knowledge. We nod our heads and think of a basic follow-up question to keep the conversation going. Not only is this the polite thing to do, but it also ties into an important social principle: people generally like to talk about themselves. Asking questions, therefore, makes people feel important. A byproduct of this is that people will perceive you to be more interesting and they may like you better.

A good baseline regarding the ratio of questions to comments is that the ratio should be even (i.e., 1:1 when possible). Of course, it varies depending on the situation (i.e., giving a speech vs. having a conversation). While having a conversation, there should be some give-and-take and some balance between questions asked and comments made. Keep in mind that a 1:1 ratio is a suggestion and not an absolute. The practical advice is for the child to learn to be aware of how much he is talking, what he is talking about, and try to find a balance between the amount of time spent talking about personal interests and the interests of others. The following strategies can assist children in this endeavor:

- Have the child audio or video record some daily conversations and then listen to the amount of questions asked and the amount of comments or statements made. Use the *Regulate > Tracking* feature on the Sōsh app to keep a tally of these while listening.
- The *Relate > Common Ground* feature of the Sōsh app encourages recognition and understanding of the interests of others in an attempt to facilitate conversations.

Open Questions

- Ask "What" to get facts (e.g., "*What did you do today?*").
- Ask "How" to process or learn more about feelings (e.g., "*How are you feeling?*").
- Ask "Why" to get reasons (e.g., "*Why did you do that?*").
- Ask "Could" to clarify the general picture of the conversation (e.g., "*Could you be more specific?*").
- Try to practice asking different questions to people while audio recording and pay attention to how others respond depending on the type of question you ask.

Closed Questions

- These usually begin with "Do," "Is," or "Are" and can usually be answered with "Yes" or "No" (e.g., "*Do you like math?*").
- Try to practice asking different questions using audio recording and pay attention to how others respond and how much information you learn depending on the type of question you ask.
- Use the Sōsh app *Tracking* feature to record the use of a particular type of question such as a Closed Question.

Paraphrasing

- Repeat back to the person a few of the main words he has said (e.g., **Person One**: "*I went to see that new 3-D movie this weekend. I really liked it.*" **Person Two**: "*It sounds like the movie was great!*").
- Audio record some of your daily conversations and then listen for paraphrasing.

Conversation Starters

This is an area in which some children feel stuck. I often hear, "I don't know what to say or how to walk up to a person and start a conversation, or how to join a conversation." There is a lot that takes place over the course of a conversation. If you are able to videotape, I encourage you to take time to "dissect" a video tape of a conversation, and notice the things that happen outside of the context of what is being said. Audio recording or speaking in front of a mirror (in the absence of a conversation partner) can provide novel learning opportunities. Some suggested conversation starters include:

- Find something about the person that you can compliment them on or that you like (e.g., "*I really like those shoes. Where did you get them?*").
- Find something in the environment around you that you can comment on (e.g., "*I can't believe how much it has been raining lately! When do you think it will end?*").
- People love to talk about themselves. Ask them questions (e.g., "*What do you do for fun?*").
- Audio record some of your daily conversations and then listen to see how you and others begin a conversation.

Many social skills approaches focus on what people should say in conversations. The problem with this is that conversations are dynamic and ever-changing. In the real world, if a person shows up for a conversation with a script, the likelihood of success is small. The conversation may move in different, unexpected directions and the individual may struggle, either trying to adhere to the script, or trying to follow the conversation. His anxiety will increase and his confidence will decrease.

It is important to remember, when coaching your child, that conversations are not always *content* heavy. Conversations can be about anything, from what is happening in the room to something that happened on the way to the conversation you are currently having. The child might even come up with an "emergency statement" to use when he is at a loss for conversation such as commenting on the weather. It is not necessary to be an expert on every topic being discussed in a particular conversation. For example, you don't need to be an expert on every baseball team and player to participate in a conversation about baseball cards. Listening, asking questions, and nodding your head in agreement are all ways of participating. It is also helpful to take something from the discussion and steer it in a direction of something that you know more about. In the example of baseball, the child could remark, "Wow, you sure know a lot about baseball cards." I like to collect things, too. My favorite thing to collect is rocks. They may not be worth as much as baseball cards, but I really enjoy adding to my collection."

Mine versus Other

The goal of this exercise is to help kids self-monitor how much they talk about their own interests during conversations and social interactions. People are more likely to focus on their personal interests during conversations if they feel nervous and want to fill space. However, they then fail to pay attention to the signals the other person sends. Eye rolling, sighing, or looking in a different direction, for example, are all indications that someone does not want to listen to a discussion about astronomy for twenty minutes. It is important for children to self-monitor and pay attention to the feedback received from others. Children with social difficulties do not do this well. In groups, I instruct participants to make an obvious gesture such as turning their chairs around or turning their heads in the opposite direction to demonstrate the lack of interest in their peer's diatribe. Over time, the child begins to pay closer attention to the more subtle cues of the peer group in an effort to avoid the dreaded "cold shoulder" treatment. Of course, we do this over-the-top body language exercise with an understanding that this is not an attempt to insult the child; it is a therapeutic exercise to be overly dramatic in our response to make an important point to help the child.

Dinner Cards/Conversation

Each of the conversation and talking strategies presented in this chapter can also be practiced and improved during daily conversations in the comfort of the family home before working to generalize these skills in real-world settings. Many families eat dinner together every evening and this is an ideal time to practice conversations (as well as table manners) with each other. This is a useful exercise even for siblings who may not have social skills difficulty. I recommend using knowledge of your family's interests when using this approach. Specifically, create a set of conversation cards to put on the table to generate conversation. The cards can have questions written on them or topics for discussion (e.g., favorite songs). You can even use "Wild Cards" that allow the person to choose their own topic of conversation. Family members can help to create these and they can be asked (e.g., what I accomplished today/this week) during every dinner time or on an as-needed basis.

Key Points

- The first step to relate is to get kids "out and about." This often requires putting behaviors (e.g., going to a social gathering) before moods (e.g., "I don't want to!") in order to make progress.

- Keep expectations low: Just attend an event!

- To facilitate interactions for young kids (18 months-kindergarten) provide opportunities to interact (e.g., arrange playdates) and be in-the-moment with the child as he navigates social interactions.

- Playdates should be brief (1 hour), with similar-aged peers, and include structured and non-structured activities.

- To facilitate interactions for older kids, select one peer to connect with initially. You can also utilize strategies like Friends Venn Diagram, calling for pizza, and calling stores.

- Many kids with social skill difficulties struggle understanding social cues, nonverbal gestures, and the meaning of idioms. Repeated exposure as well as references (i.e., Sōsh mobile app *What did That Mean?* feature) can assist in increasing understanding.

- Specific conversation skills are important (e.g., eye contact), but they must be practiced in real life settings.

- Conversations should include a similar number of comments and questions and individuals should listen as much as they talk. Specific talking strategies are referenced throughout the chapter.

Chapter Four

Relax: Reduce Stress

Relax: Reduce Stress

When I first met Jacob, he was a shy 6-year-old boy. He was hesitant to play with the toys in my office and needed his mother's reassurance for most of our time together. However, when I was able to engage him using facial expressions and humor his affect was bright and he enjoyed the interaction. He giggled and continued to initiate contact with me. Prior to the appointment, I observed Jacob in the waiting area of my office engaging his mother in a fluid back-and-forth conversation with elaborate speech. However, the first time Jacob had spoken with another child at school was the preceding Friday, although he had been in school for several months.

Jacob's mother informed me that other parents often interpret his behavior as "rude" because he will not say hello to them when they greet him. At school, he sits off by himself and plays alone, although he is very comfortable with other kids when he is away from school. Presently, at least one child is teasing him because he is not talking in school. His family is beginning to encourage more play dates at home with various children in an effort to increase his comfort level when around other kids.

When Jacob is angry or frustrated he often hides and becomes tearful. He becomes most upset if something does not go his way or if he is unable to complete a task the first time. The school is currently removing privileges for the times in which Jacob refuses to complete his work. Although his behavior appears to be oppositional or defiant at school, the majority of his difficulties seem to be related to his lack of verbal communication. His expressive speech is only limited in the school environment, though, which is indicative of underlying anxiety and social discomfort, especially around non-family members.

As with Jacob, stress, worry, and anxiety affect us all at one time or another. It may be a mild stressor, like being late to work or a more severe stressor like losing a job. Some people have a physiological predisposition toward anxiety, creating more generalized anxiety or higher amounts of anxiety in their daily lives. Stress is expressed in many forms including sweating, shortness of breath, avoidance, and even sheer terror. Children as young as Jacob express feelings of anxiety in a variety of ways such as not speaking, avoiding situations, poor sleep, or physical symptoms like stomach aches and headaches. How children cope with this stress or anxiety is critically important, given that the above symptoms can derail progress and increase stress.

Approach-Avoidance Cycle

At no time is anxiety more apparent in my private practice work than immediately preceding and during the initial social skills group meetings. This makes sense as most of us experience some uneasiness when entering a new or unfamiliar situation. There is a certain level of excitement and hesitation as we approach the unknown. However, I have periodically come across a participant who arrives at the group and refuses to enter the group due to anxiety. Some of these individuals allow me to facilitate their transition into the group, and take a "leap of faith" of sorts. We get started and everything falls into place. Others do not enter willingly. They go into lockdown mode and begin to plead with their parent or caregiver to bail them out.

I am always dumbfounded when a parent allows a child to withdraw from the social group because of this initial discomfort. This one action will have a significant effect on the child's future functioning. The impact may not be directly related to the social skills group situation, but this pervasive pattern of approaching a desired situation (i.e., wanting to attend a social group to learn how to make more friends) and then avoiding it (i.e., leaving the group) can significantly contribute to the child's ongoing difficulties. What this family has just reinforced is the notion that when things are a little uncomfortable the way to cope is to retreat and abandon the task or activity.

The initial sense of relief that may result from avoiding the anxiety-provoking situation is short-lived. Over time the child can begin to generalize this fear and lose sight of what was feared in the first place. In the area of social interactions there is plenty to be nervous about, especially if you want to connect with others but cannot figure out how to accomplish this goal. Franklin D. Roosevelt said in his Inaugural Address, "The only thing we have to fear is fear itself." What begins with avoidance as a means of coping quickly becomes comfort in the avoidance. The child learns: If I avoid social situations then I won't be uncomfortable. True, perhaps, but then he also won't be able to be social or interact with others. Fear is something we all deal with - whether it is something as seemingly small as the fear of not being liked or as significant as fearing for our lives. Being able to cope and act in the face of fear builds character and strength. Shrinking or retreating in the face of fear only leaves us immobilized and powerless. Courage is not a lack of fear, but rather it is taking action in the face of and despite the fear. The goal is to experience the feeling of worry or fear and approach the situation anyway. This is the essence of exposure, or putting oneself in unfamiliar or uncomfortable situations, which is an essential element of social skills development. In the long term, this confrontation of fear will lead to the most progress.

Sensory Breaks

Kids who experience sensory overload, anxiety, or focus/concentration difficulties throughout the day need breaks. The purpose of the break is to shift focus from one activity to another, more relaxing activity. These breaks are sometimes referred to as sensory or attention breaks. Depending on the child's unique profile, these breaks can be mandatory or used by the child as needed. Some children benefit from a break as frequent as every fifteen to twenty minutes while others need a break every ninety minutes depending on the environment (school, home, structured activity or therapy). Further, some kids benefit from beginning their day with a "sensory diet" that involves some physical activity or task (e.g., jumping on a trampoline or carrying some heavy items in a backpack) that helps the child regulate himself and get the day off to a good start *before* problems arise. Indeed, even something as simple as 15 minutes in the gymnasium with a teacher before going to the first class or activity of the day can make a difference, depending on the needs of the child.

Whenever other kids are present, consider offering sensory breaks that are disguised as other activities, especially to alleviate possible resentment from classmates who do not get breaks or possible embarrassment on behalf of the child who needs the break. These breaks should not interfere with the child's daily activities, especially in school. Thus, some creativity is necessary to determine what options for breaks are available. Examples of sensory break activities include sharpening a pencil, getting a drink of water, going to the bathroom, taking a note to the principal's office (even if the note is blank *wink *wink), or running an errand for the teacher (e.g., returning books to the school library). Notice that each of these only takes about two minutes to complete, which is the goal. We don't want the child off wandering or taking a leisurely break with no consideration of what task they vacated and need to rejoin. Once the break is completed, the child is expected to return to the task at hand. Setting clear rules and parameters around the use of these breaks can help to avoid any possible stalling (e.g., dawdling in the bathroom) or difficulty returning to the task. Sensory breaks can also be part of the child's Individualized Education Program (IEP), if applicable, and include time with the school occupational therapist or in the sensory room to jump, swing, or complete other activities.

Although some parents and teachers may initially perceive breaks throughout the day as "disruptive," forcing the child to sustain focus and attention without a break often proves to be more disruptive and anxiety-provoking. For example, let's say that you want the child to complete his homework within an hour. Some parents worry that giving the child a break every 10-15 minutes might interfere with the child's ability to complete his work in the desired hour. However, not giving the child these periodic breaks may result in fatigue and frustration that ultimately results in the homework taking significantly longer than an hour to complete.

Special Assignments/Jobs/Duties

This approach is related to sensory breaks, but can be especially useful for kids who are beginning to fear going to school, for whatever reason. Children that are hesitant to attend school or connect with others while at school can often feel a sense of empowerment when they are given a job in school or special assignment. Determine what the child's interests are and use them to help the child engage in school. For the anxious child who is not excited about going to school, we might find a task for him to complete as soon as he arrives at school, such as helping in the front office. This not only gets the child to school (i.e., gives him something to look forward to that he knows he can do well), but it also allows him some time to "warm up" to the school environment and integrate into the daily activities. Other examples may include helping clean up around the school, running errands for the teachers, working in the school library, helping front office staff, or taking the chairs off all the desks in the classroom before the other students arrive.

Children with social difficulties can also be encouraged to be "detectives" or "explorers" in their school and observe and gather data about what is happening. Thus, if a child is not yet comfortable interacting, he might feel more comfortable gathering information on how to interact from a distance. This is a sharp contrast to the child who does not know how to interact but instead of learning from a distance goes into his own world and avoids people altogether. Of course, the child needs an adult contact person such as a teacher, classroom aide, or therapist with whom to share these notes and observations. Depending on the peer group, this contact person might also be another child. Beyond a simple discussion of the "Wh" questions (e.g., "What did you see?" "Why do you think she said that?"), converting this data into exercises and goals for future interactive exercises will push the child to the next and necessary level of social skills development. For example, a child (with the help of an adult) may spend a few minutes during recess tallying how many times a peer asks a question of another peer. Or, perhaps the child watches specifically for how many times his peers look each other in the eye or take turns while playing a game. Kids are curious by nature and the detective approach is a great way to harness this trait in a manner that supports social skills development.

One important note is that this section is designed for kids who may be hesitant to attend school, whom I often refer to as the school "avoiders." These are kids that stall their morning routines or have trouble falling asleep on Sunday nights, but are still willing to go to school. Other children reach their self-reported "point of no return" and absolutely refuse to go to school; the school "refuser." The strategies in these sections will not apply to the school "refuser" but can really help with a school "avoider." If you are in a situation with a child who is approaching school refusal or you are already there, I encourage you to immediately consult with a psychologist with expertise in this area given the complexity involved in getting a child to return to school.

Allow "Buffers" and Consider Sensory Profiles

Children who are sensitive to lights, sounds, physical touch, or other sensory experiences need assistance desensitizing themselves to the stimuli that exacerbate their sensory profile. Many schools now have sensory rooms where children can swing or jump on a trampoline, for example. Parents are even becoming savvier by purchasing these items for their homes or investing in weighted blankets or vests. Noise reducing or canceling headphones or ear plugs can help to drown out noise as can soft music on an iPod. The Sōsh app has a feature called *Block Out* that has some relaxing and sensory buffering sounds such as waves and soft guitar, and also will allow individuals to customize what they want to hear from their own sound/music library. As always, creativity is encouraged and a skilled occupational therapist can direct you on strategies and resources tailored to your child who may be experiencing sensory reactivity.

Relax Time

Unlike a time-out, "Relax Time" (or any term you and your child prefer to alert the child to complete this exercise) is voluntary. Children are prompted to request a relax time during situations that elicit feelings of stress, frustration, or anger. Whether at home or school, this time might follow periods of sustained activity or work that was difficult, or after a verbal disagreement with a peer. Relax time involves the child removing himself from the situation to a specified area (e.g., a different table, a bean bag, or the child's desk). During relax time, kids may engage in one of several behaviors (e.g., read, draw, listen to music, sit quietly, or practice relaxation strategies like progressive muscle relaxation). These behaviors are individualized for each child and are intended to be self-calming strategies. Relax time lasts from 2-10 minutes, depending on the child's needs and the frequency of relax time requests. I recommend setting a timer to let the child know when relax time is over. The child (in conjunction with the adult) determines the best way to utilize this time. The child may retreat to the designated area where he can sit on pillows or in a bean bag while he quietly looks at books, hold a comforting object, or listen to music on headphones at a low volume. The specific procedure and activities available to the child can be determined on an individual basis.

Despite the concern that children may attempt to use relax time as a way to avoid non-preferred activities, experience shows that most students do not choose to remain in relax time for more than 2-5 minutes. Many then realize that they are missing some activity and choose to reengage. Any child who may be an exception, and who uses relax times as a means of avoidance, would benefit from some additional limits placed around the relax time. The number of times per day may be discussed and role plays about how to use relax time can help explain its proper use. You can also consider offering a reward when the child finishes using a relax time appropriately or in a self-directed fashion. This reward might be used either when first beginning to use the relax time procedure or intermittently in order to keep the child's interest in its continued use high.

Children should be encouraged to monitor their stress level and request these relax time breaks as needed. Sometimes visuals cards in the color red can be a way of the child telling a teacher they need a relax time without having to "make a scene" in front of the peer group to communicate the same message. Allowing the child a fixed amount of cards to use each day may help with the concern about abusing the privilege. While children are encouraged to recognize when to use one of these breaks, adults need to monitor the appropriate use of the time so that the child is relaxing and not using the time for other activities.

The goal of relax time is to teach children to briefly remove themselves from frustrating situations before they act out (i.e., stop and think), and to learn self-calming skills. Children plan where they will take relax times and what they will do during relax times, and can role-play the relax time procedure with parents, teachers, or therapists as needed before using this strategy to ensure appropriate use.

School-Wide Relaxation Program

I have observed and worked in schools where they encourage morning stretching and physical activity (e.g., walking around the gym, doing standing pushups against the wall) as well as mid-morning and afternoon relaxation breaks. Children in these schools have reported to me that they feel less stress as it provides them an opportunity to slow down and breathe, as well as regain focus, in the middle of some hard work. There are specific relaxation protocols readily available online for schools and families. I like to use kid-friendly muscle relaxation strategies such as asking the child to pretend he is squeezing a lemon in his hands and then letting go or that he is squishing his toes in mud. In the absence of a specific protocol, simply turning off the bright and buzzing fluorescent overhead lights, having kids close their eyes (perhaps even spread out and lay on blankets or towels), and listen to some relaxing instrumental music for about five minutes can do the trick. I like the idea of a school-wide relaxation time as well as a specified relaxation time for the entire family as it will reduce the overall stress level in the child's environment. To ensure that it will happen, it must be added to the daily schedule. I find that only targeting and reducing a particular child's stress level and then reintroducing them into a group of tense or stressed peers or family members is counterproductive.

Allow Down Time After School

If a child has a social skills difficulty, he is likely experiencing stress throughout the day, especially if he is school age. One of the many reasons why I am such a proponent of schools expanding their focus to help children with social difficulties is that many of these children work very hard to isolate themselves outside of school and thus the school day provides the only opportunity for them to observe and participate in social interactions. I often explain to parents that although their child may be intellectually keeping up in school, he is working at least twice as hard as the peer group to keep up with the social demands. As social interactions become more complex, beginning in the late elementary school and middle school years, the stress of trying to keep up with the peer group begins to take a toll on academics. This is in sharp contrast to the kids in the peer group who intuitively know how to be social with each other and thus their primary focus can remain on academics. A child with social skills difficulties not only has to learn new academic material throughout the day, but also needs to figure out how to relate to others and keep up with social demands. This requires tremendous energy and is taxing both emotionally and physically.

Further, children with social skills difficulties do not do well decompressing and are unable to "vent" throughout the day. The result is a child who is "carrying around" a large volume of stress at the end of the school day. Parents often feel that they are doing something wrong because their child may behave quite appropriately and "keep it together" throughout the school day and then come home and fall apart. Indeed, many children tantrum, melt down, or isolate themselves once they are in the familiar and comfortable home environment where it is safe to do so.

Thus, I strongly recommend that children be allowed immediate downtime after school and prior to the participation in any structured activities or completion of homework. The time needed to accomplish a release of stress varies from child to child. Some children require prompting or a mandatory quiet or relaxation time after school. Parents may also want to put restrictions on what the child chooses to do during this time. Playing challenging video games or those with violent content, for example, can add to the child's stress despite their insistence that games are "relaxing" or "fun." Watching a child throw a game controller across the room in frustration may serve as the necessary illustration that this activity is far from relaxing for the child. I suggest alternate activities such as reading an enjoyable book, playing with a favorite toy, watching a favorite age-appropriate TV show, listening to music, or light exercise. The choice of a screen time activity as a relaxation activity is only acceptable if the child can transition away from this activity without increasing their stress level again (i.e., tantrum), otherwise it defeats the purpose.

Exercise

Exercise is one of the most effective ways to cope with the pressures and anxieties of life. It slows the physical and mental toll that stress can take on our bodies. Happiness experts theorize that exercise may be the most effective instant happiness booster of all activities (e.g., Lyubomirsky, 2008). A Duke University study (Blumenthal et al., 2007) found exercise to be generally as effective as medication for treating depression. Even if you are not depressed or stressed, exercise is guaranteed to contribute to the overall feeling of happiness. Physical activity, exercise, intellectual prowess, and even creativity go hand-in-hand. Exercise affects the brain by building neural connections in the parts of the brain responsible for memory and "executive function," the brain regions that help kids plan and direct their actions (to be discussed further in the **Reason** chapter). They especially need this executive function in school to control their impulses, organize their homework, and, of course, to get their work done. Even when increasing kids' physical activity results in less time spent in the classroom, their intelligence and school performance improves. This illustrates the need to send our kids outside to be active more often—and that we should go with them!

Exercise does not always involve expensive equipment or workout clothes. Play can be exercise for both the child and parents, especially in rough-and-tumble form or during games of tag or chase. As children grow older, physical play is often highly dependent on physical prowess and coordination, which may deter some children from engaging in physical play. Having difficulty in the social skills domain may coincide with motor coordination difficulties that, as a byproduct, can interfere with the ability to physically interact with others or exercise, thus interfering with the ability to socialize and relax.

In other words, if the way to connect with your peers is by playing soccer with them during recess, but you aren't very good at soccer, then you must find another time, place, and activity to connect with them. Children who have coordination difficulties such as running or kicking a ball are not likely to be readily included in the daily recess soccer game. Further, the other kids may encourage the child to leave the game and tell him how "awful" he is at playing the game. Indeed, recess can be a highly stressful time of day for kids, especially because recess is generally not well structured or supervised, and aggressive or insulting behaviors often go unchecked. Thus, coordination difficulties may need to be accommodated and addressed. In the meantime, the child can find a physical outlet that does not involve as much coordination such as walking around, swinging, or bouncing a ball to help alleviate some stress.

Schools across this country are beginning to participate in physical activity initiatives. In Michigan, for example, many elementary school students participate in walking programs that reward the children with prizes such as key chains in the shape of feet for the amount of steps or laps they walk in a day. The kids enjoy collecting these and linking the key rings together as a way of displaying how hard they have worked. Whether the children walk individually or in groups, these programs are another way in which children learn more than just academics inside the four walls of their schools. Parents can also encourage this by using a pedometer and creating a reward program that corresponds to number of steps walked each day. There are also a variety of mobile apps that track physical activity and make the process interactive and fun.

For children who view exercise as "work," consider making it part of a daily family routine. Taking the dog for a family walk or going out to play ball after dinner as a family can be a fun activity and can create some fond memories. Depending on where you live, the opportunity to participate in outdoor activity may be seasonal. If your children are younger (or older and more tolerant), plugging an iPod into external speakers and dancing around the living room as a family for a few songs can be a very fun exercise. The more you camouflage the exercise component of it, the more willing the child may be to participate. Another approach is to ask that the child be active for 3-5 songs on his iPod before being allowed to sit on the couch for any extended period of time. By the time those songs have finished playing, the child has exercised for about 15-20 minutes and the music distracted his focus from the physical aspect of the exercise.

Muscle Relaxation/Breathing

Progressive Muscle Relaxation (PMR) is a technique for reducing anxiety by alternately tensing and relaxing the muscles (Jacobson, 1938). It was developed by American physician Edmund Jacobson, who realized that since muscle tension accompanies anxiety a person can reduce his anxiety by learning how to relax the muscular tension. PMR involves both a physical and mental component.

The physical component involves the tensing and relaxing of muscle groups of the legs, abdomen, chest, arms, and face. With the eyes closed and in a sequential pattern, a given muscle group is purposefully tensed for approximately 10 seconds and then released, or relaxed, for 20 seconds before continuing with the next muscle group. There are various kid-friendly approaches to PMR that are readily available online. These utilize the same muscle groups, but add kid-friendly language such as "pretend you are squeezing a lemon in your hand."

The mental component focuses on the difference between the feelings of the tension and relaxation. Because the eyes are closed, the focus is on the *sensations* of tension and relaxation. The minds of children with anxiety often wander to thoughts such as, "I don't know if this will work!" or "Am I feeling it yet?" If this is the case, the child is instructed to simply concentrate on the feelings of the tensed muscle. Because the feelings of warmth and heaviness are felt in the relaxed muscle after it is tensed, a mental form of relaxation is experienced as a result. With practice, the individual learns how to effectively relax and deter anxiety before it reaches an unhealthy level where a tantrum or panicked response could occur.

In addition to muscle relaxation, breathing is a simple but very effective method of relaxation. It is a core component of everything from a "take ten deep breaths" approach to calming someone down, right through to yoga relaxation, Mindfulness training, and Zen or Transcendental Meditation. Deep breathing works well in conjunction with other relaxation techniques such as Progressive Muscle Relaxation, relaxation imagery, and meditation to reduce stress. To use the technique, take a number of deep breaths in and out and relax your body further with each breathing cycle. Close your eyes and breathe in slowly through your nose and exhale through your mouth. Try to clear your mind of any negative or stressful thoughts each time you exhale and be patient to allow enough breaths until you feel calm and relaxed enough to stop the exercise. The Sōsh app contains a *Deep Breathing* feature to guide you through the entire exercise if you need additional assistance.

Imagine/Guided Imagery

Guided Imagery is a convenient and simple relaxation technique that can help to quickly and easily manage stress and reduce tension in the body. This approach is similar to engaging in a vivid daydream and, with practice, can help a person to relax and let go of the worries and stressors of a particular day or event. The following describes how to get started with guided imagery.

Get into a comfortable position. If a lying down position might put you to sleep, opt for a cross-legged position, or recline in a comfortable chair. Use slow, deep breathing and close your eyes, focusing on breathing in through the nose and exhaling stress and tension through the mouth.

Once a relaxed feeling has been achieved, begin to envision yourself in the most relaxing environment you can imagine. For some, this might be floating on a raft in the cool, clear waters near a remote tropical island as a gentle, warm breeze blows across your face. For others, this might be sitting by a fire in a secluded snow cabin, deep in the woods, sipping hot cocoa and reading a favorite novel while wrapped in a plush blanket and fuzzy slippers. Kids may imagine themselves in a candy store, playing with their favorite toy or family pet, or engaging in their favorite activity.

As the scene unfolds in your imagination, try to involve all of your senses. What does it look like? How does it feel? What smells are involved? What can you hear? Can you smell the salt in the air if you imagine a beach scene? Do you hear the crackle of logs on a fire, the splash of a waterfall, or the sounds of birds? Make your vision so real you can taste it, feel it and live it.

Stay in your imaginary relaxation paradise for as long as you like. Enjoy your "surroundings" and let yourself be far from whatever creates stress for you throughout the day. When you are ready to come back to reality, count back from ten or twenty, and tell yourself that when you get to one, you will feel serene and alert, and enjoy the rest of your day. When you "return," you will feel more calm and refreshed, like returning from a mini-vacation without having to leave the room. As with anything that you want to be good at, this takes practice and patience. Some people have a difficult time performing this exercise based on written instructions and prefer spoken instructions. If you need guidance on how to do this as you are going through the exercise, the Sōsh mobile app has a guided imagery audio feature, called *Imagine*, to help you.

Medications

My treatment approach as a psychologist is to intervene with behavioral and psychological approaches whenever possible before considering whether a medication consult with a physician may be warranted. However, there are some children who do not respond to sustained behavioral attempts and strategies that would otherwise be effective. There are also children who are hard-wired to be physiologically anxious and experience anxiety even in the absence of environmental triggers. In these instances, a medication consult with a qualified physician is indicated to determine if medication may help the child relax enough to accomplish his goals. Medication, when used properly, should not alter the personality nor should it create significant side effects. A developmental and behavioral pediatrician may be the ideal physician specialty to help with a medication prescription because they have the necessary training to understand the behavioral aspect as well as the physical and medical aspects of the symptom pattern. A good starting point in the process is usually your primary care physician or pediatrician before determining the need to consult with a specialist.

Physical Manifestations of Stress, Worry, and Anxiety

Somatic symptoms are physical symptoms that occur within the body. Some common examples are headaches, stomach aches, lack of appetite, and sleep difficulty. When these issues do not have a biological origin in children, they can be labeled "psychosomatic," or relating to a disorder having physical symptoms but originating from mental or emotional causes. In other words, children will often have presenting symptoms that could be consistent with a physical illness, but in reality they are dealing with the effects of emotional turmoil. The good news is that these physical manifestations provide us with observable indicators of the child's stress level and can often be easily addressed with the relaxation strategies described throughout this chapter. You are always encouraged to meet with your primary care physician or pediatrician when the child initially complains of these symptoms and then follow up with a mental health professional if it is determined that the symptoms have no physical basis.

Sleep

Lack of sleep can cause problems with many aspects of bodily and mental function. There are several ways to prevent and treat these issues so that a person can sleep better, which in turn will have reducing effects on anxiety.

Children need plenty of sleep. Average daily recommendations for sleep amounts are as follows:

- 3 to 5 year-olds = 11-13 hours (may include an afternoon nap)
- 5 to 12 year-olds = 10-11 hours
- 13 to 18 year-olds = 8.5 – 10 hours.

Not getting enough sleep can lead to anxiety because a person often worries about not sleeping enough or falling asleep and his mind races as he lays in bed trying to fall asleep. This may be especially true for children who are not feeling comfortable in school and begin to have difficulty falling asleep on Sunday evenings. Spending less time in rapid eye movement (REM) sleep can make anxiety worse, since this is the time when the body and brain are restoring themselves and rejuvenating for the next day.

There are many ways to prevent the anxiety that results from insufficient sleep. Many relaxation techniques, including those discussed in this chapter, can aid in this process (e.g., meditation, exercise, yoga, Tai Chi, music, and deep breathing). Having a relaxing bedtime routine is also important. This can include a bath, listening to music, or reading a book. People are cautioned to use their beds only for sleeping so their body will associate the bed only with sleep rather than a place where they lie awake trying to resolve issues that make them anxious. Thus, homework, reading enjoyable books, or playing portable video game systems should not be completed in bed. Some doctors will recommend using a Melatonin supplement to help with sleep, but you are encouraged to consult with your physician before using this or any other supplement.

Key Points

- The approach-avoidance cycle is a behavioral pattern of approaching a desired situation (e.g., wanting to attend a social group to learn how to make more friends) and then avoiding it (e.g., leaving the group) to alleviate anxiety. This can severely limit progress in social skills development.

- Kids who experience any sensory overload, anxiety, or focus/concentration difficulties throughout the school day need to take sensory breaks. Examples may include sharpening a pencil, getting a drink of water, going to the bathroom, or taking a note to the principal's office.

- Children may need to utilize "relax time" when they feel stressed, frustrated or angry. This time allows the child to remove himself from the situation to a specified area and regroup.

- At home, children should be allowed downtime immediately after the school day to release the stress that has built up throughout the day.

- Physical exercise is a natural "happiness booster." Encouraging kids (and the family) to be active can decrease stress.

- Other ways to decrease stress include deep breathing, progressive muscle relaxation, and guided imagery.

- Medications may be necessary to alleviate physiological anxiety, such as panic, although behavioral methods can often be sufficiently effective to avoid the need for medications.

- Pay attention to physical symptoms (e.g., headaches, stomach aches) as possible indications of emotional stress and thus a need for relaxation.

- Monitor sleep habits and use strategies to improve sleep hygiene given the importance of sleep and the significant effect of sleep on mood and energy.

Chapter Five

Reason: Think It Through

Reason: Think It Through

Aidan, an 11-year-old boy, loves his TV shows. His parents do a nice job of keeping him busy with various activities throughout the week and have a rule that Aidan must finish homework before he is allowed to watch TV. He follows this rule. Another household rule is that he cannot watch more than 90 minutes of TV each school day. By the time he finishes his homework, eats dinner with his family, and completes his after school activity, he is usually free to watch TV beginning at 8 pm and he needs to be in bed at 9:30 pm each evening. Aidan has difficulty transitioning away from the TV at bedtime and becomes very upset when he is required to do so. His frustration could be classified as a tantrum and recently he has spoken disrespectfully to his mother, including profanity that he hears his peers use at school. This is quite stressful for the family, and his parents are having a difficult time remaining calm during these exchanges. They accuse each other of handling the situation incorrectly or of creating the situation in the first place by being "too lenient" with Aidan. As a result, Aidan's transitional difficulties and behavioral outbursts have begun to take a toll on the parents' marriage. Aidan's mother finds herself dealing with most of the parenting during the evening while Dad is busy with work he has brought home. Dad, however, still offers his feedback from afar, often playing the "armchair quarterback."

Reason has to do with comprehension, inference, and thinking. Many children have difficulties in these areas until they develop the cognitive capacity to complete such mental tasks. Individuals with social difficulties typically struggle with reasoning (or thinking things through) when faced with challenging or unfamiliar situations. Responses can be strong and emotions may be out of proportion with the precipitating event. Thus, while logic could be useful in these situations, the child has not yet learned how to apply the necessary logic. Instead, logic is applied to topics of intellectual interest (e.g., why two countries went to war) more often than everyday situations (e.g., why humming in class causes others to become annoyed).

Reasoning difficulties can be linked to executive functioning problems. The term "executive function" is used by psychologists and neuroscientists to describe a loosely defined collection of brain processes. Controlled by the frontal lobe of the brain, located behind the forehead, executive functions are responsible for planning, cognitive flexibility, abstract thinking, initiating appropriate actions (e.g., starting school work without prompting), and inhibiting inappropriate actions (e.g., refraining from hitting someone when upset). Invariably, children with neurodevelopmental delays or diagnoses such as Autism Spectrum Disorders, Attention-Deficit Disorders, and Learning Disorders share executive functioning difficulties.

The frontal lobe is the "Chief Executive Officer" or "CEO" of the brain and is responsible for mediating ancillary brain processes. Think of a ball rolling into the street. First, the child's visual cortex sees the ball go into the street, and the motor cortex prepares the legs and arms to move so that the child can run after it. The frontal lobe's job in this example is to tell the child, via a thought process, "Wait! Look both ways! There might be a car approaching!" When this system is underdeveloped, these messages may get through too late or may not get through at all, and responses are based on impulses rather than thoughts. The current neurological consensus is that the frontal lobe is not fully developed until a person reaches their mid-20's, which may explain the impulsiveness and poor decision making often present among young adults. It may also explain some of the frustration associated with trying to teach various social skills, which are dependent on frontal lobe development, to children.

Video Modeling

Video modeling is a powerful tool that can be used to enhance problem solving capabilities using a modality that resonates with kids. Children with social skills difficulties often struggle to identify problems, formulate possible choices and associated consequences, choose the best solution, and implement that solution. Through video modeling, scenarios of typical problems can be created and acted out. Later, these models can be viewed and analyzed by the child (or children) and adult who is facilitating the exercise.

An example exercise is to give children a "script" for a common situation (e.g., playing together at recess). Kids are first given a description of the task or situation that is to be recorded before taping begins. The adult should model the scene for the child(ren) to provide additional preparation (i.e., use the *See One* approach). For example, the adult models how to walk up to a group of kids and ask if he can play with them. Children can then reenact the situation (while being video taped) with variations on verbal and behavioral choices and associated consequences. In this example, the peers say "sure" in one instance and begin to play with the boy who approached them. During the next scene, the outcome is that the kids tell the child that he is not welcome to play. The boy must then proceed with a problem solving approach. Participants view the video and provide feedback. For instance, the adult facilitator can ask children to first identify the problem (i.e., the boy is not allowed to play or the boy was rude when asking to join in the play). They can then be asked to generate solutions and recognize the associated consequences (e.g., How could the boy respond better/worse? What would happen if the boy responded that way? How could the boy ask differently to join the play?).

Finally, children watch to see how the "actors" chose to problem solve and observe the actual consequences recorded on video. This exercise is ideal for kids who have access to positive peer supports and mentors who can serve as the other "actors" in these scenes. If this activity is completed at home, then siblings, family members, and neighbors may take part and role play. Although the exercise is designed to help the child in question improve his social skills, the group does not need to know this and can see this as simply an acting exercise. Besides, these role plays enhance social skills and can be valuable even for the peer supports.

As discussed previously, providing live, in-the-moment coaching for individuals experiencing social skills difficulties is essential for success and generalized, sustained learning. Thus, a more powerful application of video modeling involves taping actual social interactions. While children can be videotaped using scripted dialogue, this exercise is preferable in more natural environments, such as during recess. Children learn to become better observers of themselves during interactions (self-monitoring) and recognize verbal and behavioral cues from other individuals. For example, a child who has difficulty with picking behaviors (e.g., tugging on his skin) or self-distracting behaviors (e.g., playing with his shoe laces) may be recorded during a block of time and then later asked to tally his behavior (e.g., "Count how many times you touch your shoe laces") while viewing the tape. The child is given a self-monitoring sheet in which a frequency count or tally of the behavior is recorded. This procedure helps children who are otherwise unwilling to participate in more traditional methods of self-monitoring to recognize their behaviors. Allowing the child time to discuss the video and his behaviors will help him to feel supported.

Transitions

Children with executive function difficulties often struggle to transition from one task or activity to another. They may, for example, yell or become upset when told it's time to leave a place or to stop an activity, such as playing a video game. There are ways to avoid this and make the transition between activities easy and smooth. In order for children to feel comfortable and remain cooperative while moving from one activity to the next, try incorporating the following strategies into your current approach.

First, remember that children need and love routine no matter how old they are. If they experience the same basic sequence each and every day, they will feel comfortable as they know what to expect. For example, if your basic routine with your toddler is to wake up, eat, get dressed, go out somewhere, and so forth, they will naturally move through their day with ease. They will even begin to remind you when it's time to go out if you are running late. I like to remind families that predictability equals tranquility.

For some children, it may be useful to write the schedule for the day on a dry erase board with information (or pictures) describing exactly what the child needs to have ready. The day will flow smoothly and the child will be calmer knowing what to expect. If you have a child three years or older who is anxious or has a neurodevelopmental difficulty, a schedule is a terrific way to help him feel calm and competent. Breaking large projects or periods of time into manageable steps helps to alleviate stress and improves activity completion. Allow a column on any schedule for "Uh-Oh!" or "Oops" scenarios when something that was scheduled does not go as planned and the child needs to be flexible and adjust accordingly. Examples of things that might go in the "Uh-Oh" column would be a substitute teacher, recess being indoors because of weather, having a pop quiz, changing the due date on an assignment or project, or having dinner out instead of at home because of last minute schedule changes. Finally, add two more columns to document how the child felt and how the "Uh-Oh" event was handled (e.g., "I didn't like the substitute at first but then she was nice" or "I used my relaxation exercises to breathe when I was upset about indoor recess").

Time	Activity	"Uh-Oh"	Feeling	Solution	Feeling
7:30 - 8:00	Eat Breakfast	Out of Pancakes	Mad	Ate toast with favorite jelly	Better/ Happy

The second area to consider is the manner in which you tell your child that it is time to move on to the next activity. Yelling from the other room is not a positive or effective way to prepare a child for a transition. A better way is to go to your child prior to the time in which you need to transition, sit next to him, enter his world, and make a comment such as: "You sure like your trains," or "What a neat idea you had to build a Lego house like this," or "I loved that book when I was young." Then say, "In 10 minutes it's going to be time to [insert activity here]." Some parents find that using a timer works well because the timer provides the reminders and alleviates battles between parent and child. The Sōsh app has a *Transition Timer* that has been specifically developed for this purpose with audio prompts and a visual display that the transition is approaching.

A five-minute or one-minute warning can also be useful. This helps to remind the child that being asked to stop and move to another activity is a matter of time running out, and not a parent trying to be "mean" or make life miserable.

If the child is in the middle of a video game, the time remaining warning given to the child should be accompanied by a reminder to save progress. For example, "We need to leave in 5 minutes, so you need to save your game progress before the game will be turned off." Of course, not allowing video games eliminates all transitional difficulties associate with them. However, if you like a good challenge you are almost assured one when trying to transition your child from a video game. There are token systems (e.g., familysafemedia.com) that you can connect to a game console that require the child to insert tokens (provided with the system) to "purchase" time for game play. He earns these tokens from you as a reward for completing tasks that you assign. The device, which is tamper proof and cannot be disabled by the child, then shuts the game console and television off when the time is expired. Children quickly learn the importance of managing their time and saving their game before the time is up. Make sure to provide your child with some unexpected rewards such as giving him additional time or tokens for future activities when he demonstrates an appropriate transition.

When the transition time has expired, begin transitioning the child. For younger children it may be useful to talk about where you're going, who you'll see, what you're doing, and so forth. This will keep him focused, help to manage any anxiety, and will build excitement and cooperation. Keep in mind that a small cohort of children may become increasingly anxious the more you "prep" them, so sometimes the best transitional strategy is to quickly get the child from "Point A" to "Point

B" to prevent additional stress and anxiety from building up. If the child whines, there may be other issues going on like hunger, fatigue, and unfamiliarity with a routine or limit setting. Stick with it as this too shall pass.

For an older child, consider the response cost method which involves the child owing the parent for any time he spends stalling, avoiding, or delaying the transition. Some parents do a minute-to-minute conversion so that each minute the child is late making the transition equals a minute off their game play the next day. Other families find that a double or even triple conversion works best (1 minute late equals 2-3 minutes loss of privilege). Do not talk to the child during this time but simply track the child's time delay making the transition and then calculate the conversion. For a child who is 10 minutes late moving from their activity to something else, they would lose 20 or 30 minutes of screen time. Of course, deducting screen time makes sense if the child was late because they would not transition away from the television. In other instances such as transitioning to get in the car in the morning and being late for school as a result, a parent might consider moving the child's bedtime up that evening (e.g., 5 minutes late to school equals 10 minutes earlier bedtime). The connection here is that the child must be too tired in the morning to get ready to leave on time and thus would benefit from some additional time to sleep.

Verbal cues are an absolute necessity when encouraging a child to transition from one activity to the next. Cueing should take place before, during, and after the transition. For example:

Before:	"After this puzzle, we'll put the pieces away so we can have lunch."
During:	"Time to put the pieces away so we can have lunch."
After:	"Nice job putting the pieces away! Now it's time for lunch."

Of course, real life does not usually happen this smoothly, and that's okay. Kids are not always going to like the fact that they have to stop something they enjoy.

Transitions will always be difficult for a young child and especially difficult for children with a neurodevelopmental difficulty. Developmentally, these children are less equipped than their "neurotypical" peer counterparts (i.e., children whose neurological development and function is progressing as expected based on developmental milestone achievements) to leave an enjoyable activity and move to a potentially less desirable one. Keep in mind that this, like any other daily interaction with a child, will be exacerbated by lack of sleep, hunger, or illness. Remember, even though your child may put up a fight, you are the one setting the rules and limits, and consistency is essential. If it's time to leave the playground and you give the direction to go, then it's time to leave the playground. If you say it (e.g., "It's time to go"), be sure to follow through on it!

If the situation escalates, some parents need to physically move their child from one location to another. During this process, physical contact can occur, such as the child hitting or kicking the parent. If enough time is available (i.e., you don't have to leave the home to be somewhere on time), this should result in an immediate time out. I would always encourage a parent to be five minutes late rather than giving in to a tantrum or being inconsistent.

Let's consider an example of trying to get out the door to school. In this example, let's assume that the child is 6 years old, has an older sibling who attends the same school, and hates having to get into the car to leave for school. He invariably kicks his mother while she fastens his seat belt across his booster seat. During the winter months, these kicks are especially painful because he wears heavy snow boots. One option is to use natural consequences and inform him that he must get into the car without shoes or socks (in the cold winter air) until he can demonstrate that he will not kick. Of course, you carry his boots and socks for him to put on once he is at school. The child can still kick without boots, it just won't hurt you as much.

Another option is to put the child in time out, although this is not fair to the older sibling who will be late for school as a result. Instead of the control battle that ensues, what if you removed yourself as the target and used a timer in your place? Set the timer for the amount of time until the car will leave and place it near the child. If the child does not yet grasp time or digital countdowns, then use a visual timer such as one of the many apps available for Apple devices (e.g., Sōsh *Transition Timer, Kid Kloc, Time Timer*). Instruct the child, in advance, that he is expected to be in the car, or walking to the car, once the timer beeps. If he is successful, then there will be a "prize" waiting for him (think of something that he loves and can only have access to once inside the car). Note: Only offer prizes during the early stages of getting the child to the car on time and then gradually replace prizes with verbal praise once the child gets into the routine. Any time that the child is late getting in the car is time that he will owe you later that day. So, you might say that for every minute late, the child loses 5 minutes of TV viewing from his one hour of allotted viewing time each afternoon.

Consider the strategy of anticipating the conflict with the child. Sit him down in advance of the transition and say, "Look. We are going to go to school in about 10 minutes. If memory serves, I know what will happen. You will get mad. I will carry you to the car. You will kick me and it will hurt and then I will be mad. Then you will cry the entire way to school. Every time you have done that in the past, you still had to go to school." You then try to predict a calmer outcome by saying, "What I hope can happen is that you get in the car and keep your feet still because it hurts me when you kick. It's okay to be mad and not want to go to school, but we *are* going. I also know that once you get there, you usually end up having at least a little fun." If the child is nervous about going to school, then the prize or motivator waiting for him in the car may not be enough. In this case, you may need to find a special job for the child that awaits him once he gets to school (e.g., getting to school 10 minutes earlier than other kids to play in the gym for a few minutes or help the teacher get the room ready). You might also prearrange with the child's teacher to have a special prize waiting for the child in the classroom if he arrives on time (for a limited period of time).

Another option is to tell the child that a special adventure awaits him on the day in which he gets into the car without a fight. You now own the child's curiosity; however, you must be patient. Once the child calls your bluff and gets into the car without incident, you must stop on the way to school that day and get him a special treat, even if it means you run a few minutes late to school. Then, when the child gets into a rhythm of getting into the car without incident, you randomly pick a day every so often (unbeknownst to the child) when you alter the driving route and make a brief stop for a treat to reinforce this appropriate behavior.

Perspective-Taking

Perspective-taking is the ability to see things from someone else's point of view. Success in social interactions requires that people "…be able to stand in the shoes of others, see the world through their eyes, empathize with what they are feeling, and attempt to think and react to the world in the same way that they think and react to the world" (Moskowitz, 2005, p. 277).

Perspective-taking is considered an important step in the cognitive development of children. Very young children don't understand that other people have different feelings and experiences from their own. Older children with social difficulties may understand this in terms of logic, but have a difficult time applying it to their everyday interactions. Still others may not fully understand perspective at all. This perspective taking ability develops over time until it becomes quite sophisticated in adults. Robert Selman (1971), a psychoanalyst, developed a five-stage model to describe the development of perspective taking. Consider the following:

> Holly is an 8-year-old girl who likes to climb trees. She is the best tree climber in the neighborhood. One day while climbing a tree she falls off the bottom branch but does not hurt herself. Her father sees her fall, and is upset. He asks her to promise not to climb trees anymore, and Holly promises.
>
> Later that day, Holly and her friends meet Sean. Sean's kitten is caught up in a tree and cannot get down. Something has to be done right away or the kitten may fall. Holly is the only one

who climbs trees well enough to reach the kitten and get it down, but she remembers her promise to her father.

If children of different ages are presented with this situation and asked such questions as, "If Holly climbs the tree, should she be punished?" "Will her father understand if she climbs the tree?" or "Will Sean understand why Holly has trouble deciding what to do?" the children will give answers relevant to their current level of cognitive development. Try posing this dilemma to your child to determine where he is functioning developmentally with regard to his own perspective-taking ability. The ages listed below for each stage below are the chronological ages in which it is expected that children will use that particular style or stage of perspective taking. Here are the typical responses of children:

- **Undifferentiated perspective-taking**
  Age: 3-6
  Description: Children recognize that the self and others can have different thoughts and feelings, but they frequently confuse the two.
  Response: The child predicts that Holly will save the kitten because she does not want it to get hurt and believes that Holly's father will feel just as she does about her climbing the tree: "Happy, he likes kittens."

- **Social-informational perspective-taking**
  Age: 5-9
  Description: Children understand that different perspectives may result because people have access to different information.
  Response: When asked how Holly's father will react when he finds out that she climbed the tree, the child responds, "If he

didn't know anything about the kitten, he would be angry. But if Holly shows him the kitten, he might change his mind."

- **Self-reflective perspective-taking**

  Age: 7-12

  Description: Children can "step in another person's shoes" and view their own thoughts, feelings, and behavior from the other person's perspective. They also recognize that others can do the same.

  Response: When asked whether Holly thinks she will be punished, the child says, "No. Holly knows that her father will understand why she climbed the tree." This response assumes that Holly's point of view is influenced by her father being able to "step in her shoes" and understand why she saved the kitten.

- **Third-party perspective-taking**

  Age: 10-15

  Description: Children can step outside a two-person situation and imagine how the self and others are viewed from the point of view of a third, impartial party.

  Response: When asked whether Holly should be punished, the child says, "No, because Holly thought it was important to save the kitten. But she also knows that her father told her not to climb the tree. So she would only think she should not be punished if she could get her father to understand why she had to climb the tree." This response steps outside the immediate situation to view both Holly's and her father's perspectives simultaneously.

- **Societal perspective-taking**

  Age: 14-Adult

  Description: Individuals understand that third-party perspective-taking can be influenced by one or more systems of larger societal values.

  Response: When asked if Holly should be punished, the individual responds, "No. The value of humane treatment of animals justifies Holly's action. Her father's appreciation of this value will lead him not to punish her."

As children mature, they consider a variety of information. They realize that different people can react differently to the same situation. They develop the ability to analyze the perspectives of several people involved in a situation from the viewpoint of an objective bystander. When intervening with children, adults typically end their statements with how the behavior affected others. For example, "You hit me, and that hurt my feelings." For children who have difficulty understanding that others feel and think differently than they do, these statements often carry very little weight. The child may understand that it is, in fact, "bad" to hurt someone's feelings, but not understand why that's the case. In addition, the child may fail to understand the social effect of his own behavior in the absence of direct feedback from others.

When we use a social feedback loop, we bring the social consequences back to the child. That is, how will hurting other people's feelings affect the child who did the hurting? For example: "When you hit Erica, you hurt her, and when you hurt people, they are not going to want to play with you anymore. When you hit people, they become afraid of you and they won't want to be your friend." This way, children see how their behavior feeds back directly to them.

Mental Strategies

Executive function is essential to success in all areas of daily functioning, not just social skills. Many parents express frustration regarding their child's apparent difficulty completing the most mundane of everyday tasks, such as getting out of bed and brushing teeth in a timely manner, despite his ability to complete these tasks. Asking the child to go to his room and get his shoes can turn into a 30-minute exercise requiring repetition of the directions. The speed that the child is able to complete activities may slow down the family or peers, who may become frustrated. Further, the child who notices these differences and compares his performance to others may experience decreased self-esteem. Regarding school functioning, any deficit in executive function will interfere with academic progress. As the demands of school increase exponentially between the fourth and seventh grades, children with executive functioning delays begin to fall behind, forget materials, and fail to turn in assignments, to list a few associated problems.

The following section is an overview of the executive functioning areas in which children may experience difficulty, as well as strategies to help. If concerned about your child's difficulties in school or completing activities of daily living, then an assessment of executive function completed by a child psychologist with expertise in this area of development is highly recommended.

Working Memory

Working Memory is your ability to hold information in your memory while completing a task. Remembering a phone number until you can write it down requires working memory. Children with working memory difficulties struggle to complete multi-step directions such as,

"Go to your room, get your coat, and put your dirty clothes in the laundry on your way downstairs" without reminders. Children with ADHD and other neurodevelopmental diagnoses often have working memory difficulties. The following strategies can help such children:

- Quietly talk yourself through a task. Referred to as subvocalizing, sometimes processing information in a soft volume (i.e., speaking "under your breath") can assist in concentration and ultimately in task completion.

- Create a written checklist of steps required to complete a task and approach larger tasks one step at a time.

- Ask others to repeat instructions or new information to assess understanding before getting started.

- Use Mnemonic devices (i.e., memory strategies) or try to combine information into chunks (e.g., instead of remembering 2, 7, and 8 separately you can memorize the numbers as "278").

- Rehearse material to help store it in your memory. This involves practicing, via repetition, the information to be retained. The more that a person practices using new information and rereads it, the more likely that it will be stored into memory.

Mental Flexibility

This is the ability to adapt or change when faced with a setback, obstacle, mistake, or new routine/task/information. Children who are considered to be mentally "inflexible" will almost always have difficulty with transitions. For example, a family goes to dinner at their favorite restaurant and the child orders his favorite bowl of soup. The waitress informs him that she is sorry, but they are out of that soup today. The child becomes angry, perhaps has a tantrum, and is seemingly unable to choose something else from the menu. This can be difficult for parents as well as the child. Consider the following strategies to help:

- Establish a daily sequence of routines (e.g., get up, brush teeth, get dressed). Document this in the most user-friendly manner (e.g., picture chart, daily planner, electronic organizer). Experiment with different ways to complete routines (e.g., try driving the child to school using various routes).

- Allow a few minutes of "down time" or relaxation between the end of one activity and the beginning of the next. This can ease the stress of transitions.

- Note any changes in scheduled activities in a daily planner or address them with a preferred problem-solving strategy.

- Develop a response for when the routine changes. The question to be answered is, "How do I plan to deal with a change I was not expecting?"

- Pay attention to others and learn how they adjust to change through observation.

- Establish an "escape plan" with the child such as a code word or signal that allows them to communicate stress associated with an unexpected change and get away for a set time period to regain composure, use relaxation strategies, etc.

Self-Monitor

This executive function is the ability to keep track of a personal behavior and the effect it has on others. This also involves recognizing and assessing your performance while completing a task or activity so that the approach can be modified accordingly. For example, task-monitoring involves recognizing when you make a mistake, such as a spelling error, and you correct it. Another example is a child who rushes his work and does not notice that he is writing an answer in the space on the page that is designated for another question.

Consider the following strategies to help:

- Encourage the child to identify his strengths and weaknesses for specific tasks or activities. Ask him to predict his performance (e.g., "How well do you think you will do?") and then complete an after-the-activity evaluation (e.g., "How well did you do?"). Create your own 5-point rating scale of how well you did, or use the Sōsh app *Rate* feature.

- Videotape an activity or situation in order to watch for specific behaviors as well as reactions to situations and interactions. For example, if a child hums during silent work in class, video record this behavior and review the footage with the child to increase awareness and negotiate replacement behaviors that may serve the same purpose (e.g., hum inside head, chew gum, use stress ball).

- When completing a task, try to ask, "What works?" and "What doesn't work?" or "What am I doing?" as self-monitoring tools.

Get Started

This is the ability to begin a task or activity in a timely manner and, ideally without much prompting or assistance. Consider the following strategies to help:

- Create "to do" lists or goals related to accomplishing activities. Topics or activities that a child finds particularly interesting will be easier to begin.

- Provide incentive or rewards to help begin tasks. For example, if the child begins homework without reminders then he can stay up an extra 15 minutes at night (or a later curfew for the older child).

- Be specific about how to begin working on a task and what steps to follow in order to overcome difficulties getting started. Break things down into manageable steps.

Control Your Behavior

The ability to stop and think before you act is essential. This involves resisting your impulses and stopping a behavior at the appropriate time. Consider the following strategies to help children with difficulties in this area:

- Utilize behavior stopping techniques. Strategies such as counting to 5 or 10 before responding or reacting to a situation can provide the necessary time to think about your response and the possible consequences.

- Identify responses that may or may not be helpful as you approach a particular task or activity. For example, it may be helpful to ask for help when frustrated or confused but it may not be helpful to crumble up your worksheet and throw it on the floor while feeling this way.

- Take periodic attention breaks (that preferably include some physical activity). Determine the most effective time intervals for taking breaks (e.g., every 10 minutes).

Manage Your Feelings

This is the ability to manage how your feelings are expressed so that you can complete a task (e.g., control your frustration so that you can finish an assignment). Consider the following strategies to help children with difficulties in this area:

- Use the Sōsh app or check in with a peer or adult to determine if your response is appropriate to the situation. This might include an adult who is available to inform the child how his behavior affected others and how that will ultimately have an effect on the child.

- Think logically about a problem as a means of keeping your emotional responses more controlled.

- Learn and practice healthy strategies (e.g., walk away, agree to disagree, take a break, deep breathing) for dealing with situations that result in strong emotions. The Sōsh app includes the *What Helps?* feature that asks the person to identify strategies that help and review them in the moment of frustration or upset.

- Consider short breaks or "calm down" periods to think about your response to an event or situation. This approach works best before frustration occurs.

- Use the *Stress* toolbar button on the Sosh app to manage your stress throughout the day and prevent an emotional "explosion." In the absence of the Sōsh app, demonstrate stress with the child by blowing into a balloon to represent their stress each time you fill the balloon with air. Note that there is only so much room for stress in the balloon before it will pop. Thus, you need to let some stress or air out occasionally before you can add more stress.

Processing Speed

This refers to the time that the brain requires to take in, understand, and respond to information. Kids with social skills difficulties may look as if they did not hear what you said to them because they are quietly thinking of a response. A child with slow processing speed may have difficulty keeping up with note taking in class, for example, and continue to write down material as the teacher moves on to the next section. Thus, content can be lost and both mental and physical fatigue is inevitable. Consider the following strategies to help such children:

- Don't be afraid to ask others to slow down, repeat the main points, or explain in more detail what they are talking about until you fully understand something.
- Make others aware of your need for extra time to process information and respond. Try telling others, "Please give me a moment to think about what you just said."
- Reduce distractions as much as possible. Use sensory buffers or other strategies to tune out environmental distractions.
- Try to plan ahead and leave as much time as possible to complete a task.
- Try to work on one task at a time.

Key Points

- **Reason** has to do with comprehension, inference, and thinking. Individuals with social difficulties typically struggle with reasoning (or thinking things through) when faced with challenging or unfamiliar situations.

- Controlled by the frontal lobe of the brain located behind the forehead, executive functions are responsible for planning, cognitive flexibility, abstract thinking, initiating appropriate actions (e.g., starting school work without prompting), and inhibiting inappropriate actions (e.g., refraining from hitting someone when upset).

- Video modeling is a powerful tool that can be used to enhance problem solving capabilities using a modality that resonates with kids. Through video modeling, scenarios of typical problems during social interactions can be created and acted out. Later, these can be viewed and analyzed by the child(ren) and the adult who is facilitating the exercise.

- Transitions are often difficult, especially among children with limited mental flexibility. Routines, structure, and predictability help to ease transitions. Rewards for successful transitions and consequences for difficulty transitioning can also be effective.

- Perspective-taking is considered an important step in the cognitive development of children. When using a social feedback loop, bring the social consequences back to the child. That is, how will hurting other people's feelings ultimately affect the child who did the hurting?

- Mental Strategies consist of a variety of tools and approaches to help a child navigate activities of daily living successfully.

Chapter Six

Regulate: Manage Behaviors

Regulate: Manage Behaviors

Jessica and her 4-year-old son, Jack drove to their first play date with one of Jessica's new "Mommy" friends, Michelle, and her 4-year-old son, Bailey. They arrived at Michelle and Bailey's home and began to play in the living room, where a variety of toys were stored. The mothers were engaged in conversation, updating one another on their lives, as the boys explored the toys. There was quite a difference, though, in how each boy proceeded. Jack picked out a toy truck and began to push it forward as he made engine noises. He placed blocks inside the back of the truck so that he could "transport" them across the room. Bailey, however, began dumping out storage bins of toys on the floor, one after the other. He seemed more excited about watching the toys fall out of the bins than how he might play with any of these items. Jack watched from a distance, puzzled as to what Bailey was doing. Jack looked over to his mother, who was well aware of the situation. Jack's mom, Jessica, looked at Bailey and then at Michelle expectantly, but Michelle continued her conversation as if Bailey's behavior was appropriate for this situation.

Once the toys were scattered throughout the room, Bailey made a game of running through the mess and even picked up several of the toys and threw them into the air. One of the toys came dangerously close to hitting Jack in the head and Jessica became increasingly uncomfortable as Michelle's only response was, "Bailey, be careful sweety." Of course, this only amused Bailey who was now throwing the toys higher into the air. Michelle did not make any additional attempts to redirect Bailey's behavior. Jack saw Bailey enjoying this type of play.

Jessica and Jack finished the play date and said their goodbyes before heading home. Following Jack's afternoon rest period, he entered the play room in his house and began to mimic the behavior he saw Bailey engaging in earlier. This was in stark contrast to Jack's typical play which is almost always regulated and consists of elaborate pretend themes such as "feeding" baby dolls and "battling" with action figures while making up stories for the characters. His mom, Jessica, quickly redirected the behavior and explained to Jack that throwing toys is dangerous and not tolerated. Jack replied, "But Bailey can do it!" Later that night, Jessica called a girlfriend to share her experience and concerns. The friends decided that since Jessica and Michelle seemed to get along well, perhaps they could get together in the future for a girls' night out, but without the kids. In this moment, Bailey lost another possible play partner due to his inappropriate behavior.

The ability to **Regulate** is the ability to adjust, control, and manage your behaviors. It is also the ability to calm yourself when excited or dysregulated, or when feedback from others suggests that you should alter your behavior in some way. This chapter is especially intended for families trying to raise children who experience behavioral difficulties that coincide with social interactional difficulties, although the information will prove useful for all parents interested in managing a child's behavior. As can be seen in the example above, a child's behavior has a ripple effect on social function. Sometimes parents become so accustomed to a child's behaviors that they don't see the need to address the behaviors, or perhaps they lack an effective approach and so they avoid any attempts to correct. If a child with social difficulties is going to make improvements in his social development, he needs other kids with whom to interact. If there are behavioral difficulties present, the child runs the risk of further distancing himself from the playmate or peer group because of the disruptive nature of the behaviors. Thus, parents need to be aware of their child's behaviors and must be willing to use behavior modification and discipline strategies both at home and while in public, as embarrassing as this may be. This way, the child learns how to interact appropriately and any observers see that the child who is having difficulty has a parent who is aware of the difficulties and is making efforts to modify the behavior.

Understanding the Behavior

Once a family is able to recognize or is willing to acknowledge that there is a behavioral difficulty occurring, the thing that I stress most often to families, and I try to get across to schools, is that behavior does *not* explain causes. What might appear to be an attention problem, distractibility, or oppositional defiance may be related to a learning difficulty, autism spectrum diagnosis, depression, anxiety, etc. Without a thorough and appropriate clinical assessment it is difficult to determine what is motivating the behavior. Schools are often quick to suggest that the child should have a medication evaluation without first performing a functional behavioral analysis and observation of what might be triggering the child's behavior in school. It is essential to do a comprehensive assessment that includes gathering home and school data, observations, history, and formal assessment such as rating scales and interactional assessments before deciding on any treatment plan.

Consider this hypothetical exercise: Enroll in an Advanced Calculus class before you learn how to add and subtract and see what happens to your behavior, your mood, and your thought process. You may begin wiggling in your seat, doodling on the page, getting up to leave, chewing on your pencil, and generally feel frustrated. Your behavior is a byproduct of your environment (this class is unfamiliar and others seem to have more of a foundation), your past experiences (you have not yet acquired the foundational knowledge to support Advanced Calculus), and what you are asking yourself to do (the content of the class is too difficult based on what you currently know). So while your behavior appears distractible and restless, it is a byproduct of the situation. Thus, if a child can sit through most other classes or activities in without any difficulty, then environmental changes can be made to assist with the behaviors in question. In the above example, this would involve dropping the advanced class and enrolling in an entry level math course to establish a foundation in the subject.

Young children who have not had many opportunities to be around other kids, or are only or firstborn children (where there is no basis for sibling comparison yet), may behave in a manner at home that, although inappropriate, does not concern the parents. Especially in the case of boys--parents, extended family, and even pediatricians in some cases look at some behaviors as, "boys will be boys" or "he will grow out of it."

Once you can accurately identify what is motivating a behavior, you can establish a plan to modify the behavior. As with any good behavioral plan, there is a high likelihood that the behaviors you are trying to stop will increase when you initially execute the plan. This is the child's way of getting the parents to "back off" or to convince the parents that their plan "does not work." Parents must dedicate the necessary time to modify behaviors and remain persistent. Once a consistent plan is established and properly executed, the hope is that the approach will become a part of everyday life.

When I hear from a parent that a plan "stopped working," it is usually a result of inconsistency or an abrupt termination in the execution of the strategy. The idea is to shift the approach permanently, not simply to utilize the plan briefly. Children will exhibit challenging behaviors throughout their childhood and adolescence. Some adults continue to exhibit challenging behaviors! The key is to establish a response style and stick with it while making slight modifications along the way that are based on the child's age and level of development. For example, a time out may be used when a toddler hits a parent, but the police may need to be called or the child may be grounded if they hit you as a teenager. There is always a response to the behavior, but the response has to be appropriate for the specific behavior and the age of the child.

Managing Difficult Behavior

If you have a child with social difficulties and are convinced that consequences don't work, or you avoid disciplining your child because you worry he doesn't understand that what he is doing is wrong, you need to read and reread this chapter. If the goal is to help the child improve his social skills, it is crucial to teach him appropriate behavior or you risk losing continued opportunities to improve social skills, much like Bailey in the earlier example. Behavior modification is the job and responsibility of any parent. This requires *action*. If a child slaps his brother, for example, saying, "Don't do that!" or "Be nice!" will *not* change the behavior.

If you believe that your child cannot help his behavior or that he doesn't mean to behave that way because he has "x" diagnosis, please accept the challenge to remain focused on the behavior itself and remember that you are working on the behavior out of love for the child and not to be mean or make the child's life more uncomfortable. Indeed, the fact is that **you love the child too much to put up with or stand idly by and watch as he exhibits inappropriate behavior**. You are never helping a child by looking the other way. I tell families that if a child is in a wheelchair and hits someone, the behavior is still hitting. I do not make exceptions; I simply look at the behavior. If you want people to respect you and spend time with you, then you cannot hit them. There needs to be a consequence for that. If your 11-month-old crawls over to your new laptop computer with a sippy cup and proceeds to dump the liquid over your keyboard, are you going to sit back, watch, and calmly say "No, sweetie," or think to yourself, "Well, he's just a baby. He doesn't know any better"? My hunch is that you would be out of your chair redirecting the child both physically (picking him up) and verbally (telling him "No") while also modifying the environment (moving the laptop computer to a different location or a tall table out of the child's reach). Direct actions and clear consequences are always the proper response.

Behavior Modification 101

Behavioral psychology focuses on how to increase or decrease behaviors by using rewards and punishment, or in "behavioral speak," reinforcement and response cost. In general, reward-based programs are more effective when modifying behaviors. There are many great resources for tracking reward programs. For example, iReward, a mobile application for Apple devices, allows a parent to document behavioral information easily and reward accordingly. A simple way to reward small children, without the use of technology, is to create a chart with the child's expected daily routine and chores (brush teeth, pick up toys) and put a sticker next to each item as it is completed. These charts can be useful when used for a brief period of time or to "jump start" a particular behavior such as brushing teeth every morning. Unfortunately, trying to keep up with paper charts often becomes difficult in the long-term.

Behaviors are often categorized as good behaviors, bad behaviors, and behaviors that can be ignored. When your child behaves well, you should react right away by rewarding him. This will guide him to behave appropriately more often. One "good" thing you can do, that does not cost you any money, is to pay attention to him. A child will work very hard to get attention from a parent. In fact, sometimes children will behave badly just to get attention! Parents often think that giving "bad" attention, like lecturing the child, will make the child behave more appropriately. However, sometimes to a child, any attention is good. This means that if you follow a bad behavior with *any* attention (like lecturing), the bad behavior might increase. Again, if a behavior (good or bad) is immediately followed by *any* type of attention, that behavior will occur more *often*.

Paying Attention

The behaviors that children engage in that we want to see more of are the "good" ones that should be reinforced. Thus, we reward those behaviors because **what you focus on expands**. Try to practice paying attention to your child and focusing on what he does that you want to see more of in the future.

Paying attention to a child is easier when they are younger and crave your attention. In order to pay attention to a child, regardless of age, you want to be in the moment with them and have your attention focused completely on what they are doing. Provide periodic comments about the behavior (e.g., "You are doing a nice job stacking those blocks" or "Wow, you are really working hard on that homework!"). For younger kids, this is accomplished by remaining in the room while they complete a task, especially during their play. As children get older and want more space, you will need to periodically check in with the child to provide reinforcing comments (i.e., peeking in the room during homework to tell them you are proud of their hard work). Avoid negative comments like,

"Oh, I see that you are not working!" Instead, watch and wait for the child to do something that you want to see more of and then make a comment (e.g., "You did a nice job getting started on your work again after that break"). Avoid asking questions, giving instructions, or guiding behavior while paying attention. Simply comment on what you see happening that you like. When you become good at this, which you will, your well-timed comments will ultimately guide the child's behavior.

Once you are comfortable with your ability to pay attention to the child, start attending to his good behaviors for the rest of the day. For example, when he is doing a chore, be sure to pay attention every so often while he's doing it (e.g., "Nice job picking up the toys in the living room"). This will make him feel better about doing the chore. It will also increase the chance of him doing things in the future without being asked. Catch him being good or doing well and let him know you noticed. Remember, in order to increase good behavior, you need to pay attention to it often and on a regular basis. Paying attention is not easy to do correctly or consistently, so practice and work hard. The results will be worth its effort.

Rewards

Reinforcement and rewards vary depending on the person. Rewards that occur immediately after a behavior are best. The longer the time between a behavior and a reward, the less effective the reward will be. Parents often ask about the best reward to use with their child. I tell parents that the best reward is anything that is potent, or meaningful, to the child. You will know quickly if this is the case because the reward will motivate future behavior. Believe it or not, many children are not motivated by money or other material rewards. As a result, it may be useful to consider the following types of rewards:

- **Social rewards** control most of our behavior. These rewards can be physical, verbal, or activity-oriented.
    - ➢ **Physical rewards** are things such as hugs, kisses, a wink, a pat on the back, or an arm over the shoulder.
    - ➢ **Verbal rewards** involve praise. Examples include:

        "I like it when you…"

        "Thanks for… "

        "You act grown up when…"

        "I'm proud of you for…"

        "You did a great job…"

    - ➢ **Activity rewards** are things you do *with* your child that he likes. Examples include:

        Playing a game.

        Reading a story.

        Going for a walk.

        Making something together.

- **Nonsocial rewards** include things such as money, toys, stickers or candy. These must be things your child likes. You should always combine verbal praise with nonsocial rewards. Nonsocial rewards should **never** replace your praise and your attention as these are most important for your child. Instead, these rewards can be used *in addition* to your praise and attention. We have to be very careful of our society's temptation to equate love with money or material gifts.

One of the most important things about giving a reward is telling your child why he's receiving it. Always tell your child exactly what he did that you liked. For example, "I am very proud of you because you did your homework without being told." Unless you tell him specifically what he did that you liked, he won't know what to do next time to be rewarded or have his behavior noticed. You could also add, "I'm going to let you stay up an extra 30 minutes tonight because of that." Indeed, what I refer to as the "When They Least Expect It" reward is especially effective. The reason for this is that kids will try to behave in a way that increases their chances of being rewarded.

Social rewards (i.e., physical, verbal, and activity rewards) are good because they don't cost any money. They can be given often and immediately after a behavior. However, it is helpful to use nonsocial rewards when you want to "jumpstart" or change a behavior. You can speed up learning by using nonsocial and social rewards together. Thus, giving a child prizes, money, or other "bribes" is an effective means to jumpstart a behavior but should not be the standard reward pattern for all behavior. Instead, always combine verbal or physical social rewards with nonsocial or material rewards. After awhile, decrease the nonsocial rewards. Praise alone should then be powerful enough to maintain the behavior.

For example, let's say a boy is having hygiene difficulty and claims that he "can't" take a shower. We can pique his interest with a $25 reward to take the first shower. He wants the money, so he showers and receives his payout, and he also demonstrates that he *can* perform the behavior. You tell him he did a "good job" taking the shower as you pay him the money. You would not want to pay him $25 for each shower from that point forward. You would either stop paying him after the first shower or reduce his payout by $5-$10 each time until he is no longer being paid and instead only receiving verbal praise for his hygiene completion (i.e., telling him he did a "nice job" and you are proud of him after he showers). I recommend using this method only for behaviors that are truly difficult for the child to begin. If you are not careful, the child will suddenly have "difficulty" getting through every aspect of his day unless he receives a little payout from mom or dad!

Toilet training is another example. We might give a piece of candy like an M & M to the child each time he sits on the potty while also praising him (e.g., "Good job!" while clapping our hands). He might get the M & M each time he sits for the first week and then he gets the M & M either randomly or at a different interval, such as every other time he sits. As the cheering and verbal praise continues and the candy reward is decreased, the child remains motivated by the praise.

Ignoring Behavior

Behaviors that are not dangerous or destructive, but are perhaps just irritating or annoying, can be ignored. Examples of these behaviors could include whining, pouting, making annoying sounds, and even having a tantrum by flopping on the floor like a rag doll. Ignoring is just the opposite of paying attention. Ignoring unimportant behaviors and paying attention to *good* behaviors with praise should all be done together. You are encouraged to practice all of these skills whenever you are with your child. When he is being good, you should pay close attention and reward him. When he is not being good, you should ignore him unless he is doing something dangerous. So, ignore irritating behavior, but start paying attention as soon as he stops acting this way and begins to behave in a more acceptable manner. By ignoring, you stop yourself from paying attention to obnoxious behaviors and therefore decrease the chances of such behaviors continuing or reoccurring.

When you are ignoring, DO NOT use any of the following:

- Eye contact
- Verbalizations
- Physical contact

In other words, you don't *look* at, *talk* to, or *touch* the child when you are ignoring him. Remember, paying attention to annoying behavior will just make it worse. To ignore, you should act like you cannot see him or hear him. You might even need to leave the room or turn your back. Be especially careful when doing this with toddlers because they have a keen sense of your behavior and will be able to detect the slightest facial grimace or glance. If they sense that you find any humor in their behavior or pay any attention to it, you have just reinforced them, which is the opposite of what you want.

It is very important that once you start ignoring a certain behavior, you keep doing so. If you don't, the child will learn that if he is bad long enough, he can get your attention. What normally happens is that when you first start ignoring a bad behavior, it gets worse. This happens because children sometimes think they're just not acting *bad enough* to get your attention. However, if you continue ignoring the behavior, it will begin to disappear. Many parents lose their patience and cave in, which is why they often report that a particular behavior plan "does not work." The plan actually *does* work, the parent just gave in too soon. If a behavior does stop, it's often fairly permanent, unless you start paying attention to that behavior again. For example, consider the parent who, upon witnessing an old behavior of concern pop up again, makes a scene in front of the child. The parent who exclaims, "Ugh! Here we go again! I thought you were not going to do that anymore!" has just breathed new life into a behavior that was recently nonexistent. The child thinks, "Oh, I'm onto something here. Look at how I got mom's attention!"

The problem for most parents who are convinced that a plan "did not work" is that they typically have a child who is very persistent and who may require an extended period of time (45 minutes to an hour) before the behavior begins to fade. The child will also likely require consistent ignoring over a period of weeks and even months to truly make the behavior go away. Unless you can "ride it out," regardless of the time this may take initially, the behavior will not go away.

Behavior modification operates much the same way as Las Vegas slot machines. Just as the slot machine will pay out often enough to keep your attention and suspense (and thus you keep playing and spending money), if a child has any indication that he will win (i.e., gain your attention) if he behaves a certain way enough times or for a long enough period of time, he will keep "pulling the lever." This is referred to as an intermittent schedule of reinforcement. That's why I tell parents you need to dedicate yourself to extinguishing this behavior by ignoring it at all costs. Otherwise, you are wasting your time and you might as well save the trouble and give in or pay attention to the behavior right away. Thus, if you have a child who likes to scream for 45 minutes when he is not getting his way, and you are stressed on a particular day and cannot ignore effectively, my advice would be to give in right away on that particular day. Otherwise, you may try to ignore the behavior but then lose your patience and give in 20 minutes into the tantrum. What you have just communicated to the child is that if his tantrum is long enough you will eventually give in. As a result, he should keep screaming until he gets his way. That's why I always say, "Give in immediately to the child's behavior or wait the child out at all costs." Of course, I think that waiting a child out is the best approach, but I also acknowledge that parents run out of energy on certain days and need to respond to the child accordingly (i.e., cut your losses and give in) on those days.

Behaviors such as physical aggression toward others (hitting, kicking, slapping, biting, spitting) and destruction of physical property obviously cannot be ignored and other procedures (e.g., time out, which will be discussed in the next section) can be used. A child who hits or bites himself but does not break skin or bones is behaving this way to gain attention and this behavior, as difficult as this sounds, would also fall into the category of ignorable behavior.

Remember:

- Ignoring a behavior (i.e., no touch, no talk, no look) will help it go away.
- When you first start ignoring a behavior, it might occur more often. If you continue ignoring it, the behavior should go away. Hold your ground!

One other effective behavioral technique, when you have a child who is behaving inappropriately and there is a sibling or other child involved, is a variation of what is referred to as Differential Reinforcement of Other Behavior or DRO. This works by rewarding the non-offending party in the presence of the offender. Thus, the sibling who remains quiet and calm while the brother or sister is having a fit or is serving a time out gets plenty of verbal praise, perhaps an extra round of a board game or other prize, all within the earshot of the sibling who is behaving inappropriately and is being ignored. This encourages the sibling who is behaving appropriately to maintain composure and not copy his brother or sister's inappropriate behavior while also alerting the offending sibling that his behavior gets him a "whole lotta nothing" and the way to get mom or dad's attention is to behave appropriately. The child who is being ignored with this strategy may initially experience a "flare up" of frustration because the sibling is getting more attention. This is okay. Ride it out because it won't be long before you realize the power of this technique and how hard the child who is misbehaving will start to work to get into that sibling's position of receiving praise and rewards. The goal is for all siblings to receive praise at the same time, so that no one is in trouble and no one is being ignored.

Aggressive, Destructive, or Dangerous Behaviors = Time Out

The types of behaviors that can never be ignored are those that are dangerous or aggressive, that hurt others, that severely hurt oneself, or result in the destruction of property. These are all instances in which the child must receive an immediate consequence that, depending on the age of the child, usually consists of a time out. There are a lot of approaches to time out with most recommending one minute spent in time out for each year of life. I advocate using a simple time out procedure. The primary goal is to send a clear message to the child that what they are doing is unacceptable and they will lose parental attention for a set period of time as a result. Thus, any dangerous behavior (hitting, kicking, biting, breaking toys or other property) results in an immediate removal from that situation. If the child is overly aggressive, trying to move him into his room may only escalate the situation. You may need to remove yourself briefly from the situation if you need to gain some composure. Whenever possible, try to direct the child to a nearby location to begin the time out. I try to not focus too much on "perfect" time out behavior and find that removal from the situation and the child losing out on interaction is what results in behavioral change over time. Thus, a few minutes away from whatever they were previously doing provides an adequate "teaching moment."

When preparing to use time out successfully, the first thing you should do is choose a time out location in your home. The ideal location is a place close to where most of the behaviors occur. It may be helpful, especially if the child responds well to visual aids, to designate the time out space in the home with masking tape, such as a rectangle on the floor or carpet. This way, the child can move freely within the space while still recognizing the boundaries. Recall that any time spent looking at, talking to, or touching the child is paying attention to the child. Time out is designed to be time <u>away</u> from any attention.

The way to ensure that the child understands the time out procedure is to play a game about time out while the child is in a good mood and is behaving appropriately. Ask the child to demonstrate a good time out in exchange for a prize (e.g., a special game with you or a treat). If the child truly does not understand time out, then you will need to demonstrate by putting yourself in "time out" while the child watches. Then ask the child to show you. Once he can do this without needing you to demonstrate or coach him, you now have the evidence that he knows how to complete a time out. Thus, when you are in the heat of the moment, you need to remember this and not talk to the child beyond directing them into time out. If you absolutely need to speak during a time out, then never do so directly to the child. If another adult is present, use what I refer to as "cross talk." An example would be the child who does not go into the desired location right away. Mom might say to her husband within earshot of the child, "Daddy, I am ready to start Billy's time as soon as he is sitting in the right spot. Once he's done with his time he can come back and play with us. I can't wait until Billy is ready to come back and play with us!"

Some parents are absolutely convinced (and then they try to convince me) that time out is not effective for their child or their child "does not care" about serving a time out. I offer these families the following responses: 1) If time out were not effective or the child did not care, then the child would be spending most of their free time in the time out area of the house; 2) If time out is "not working" with the child, then someone is paying attention to the child (e.g., talking, looking, touching while redirecting to sit down, or even sitting outside of a room to keep the door from being opened) while the child is serving his time out, and 3) If time out is "not working" then it has not been used at the right time (i.e., immediately following the behavior) or enough times and on a consistent enough basis to change the behavior.

Regarding the latter point, some parents seem to be convinced that time out should be the "magical" consequence that will radically transform the child's future behavior (i.e., thinking, "My child will hate time out so much that he will never want to have another one and thus he will never misbehave that way again"). Unfortunately, parenting is about repetition, especially if the child is younger, which also happens to be the most appropriate time to use time out with a child. Kids need reminders and do not yet have the cognitive capacity to quickly learn from mistakes or even reason through possible consequences for their behavior. Recall the **Development** chapter which emphasized that kids generally learn best from repeated, in-the-moment experiences. Thus, it is our responsibility as parents to teach them through repetition and consistency. Think of it this way: each time you use time out is a learning opportunity for the child, *not* a reminder that things are not working.

Now you need to know the best way to start a time out. As an example, let's say that you have decided to use time out for hitting. What should you do once your child hits?

Steps for effective time-out:

- Tell your child, "We do NOT hit. Because you hit, you have to take a time out" (I like the phrase, "Because you hit, you must sit"). You should say this only once. Say it in a calm but firm and authoritative voice. Be sure to use a matter-of-fact voice that differs from your "Sweety, can I have a hug?" tone. The child needs to know that you mean business, but your tone should not be angry (or soft and sweet) but rather, firm. No more speaking is required.

- Do NOT lecture, scold, or argue. Do NOT accept any excuses. Ignore shouting, protesting, and promises to be good. Direct the child to the time out location. You may need to move him physically (e.g., carry him), but avoid this when possible.

- After about two minutes of time spent in the time out area, tell him he can get up. Don't get caught up on starting and stopping a timer for noises made, etc. As long as the child is in the designated area and is not speaking inappropriately, then the time can start. If you use time out frequently, you can estimate the time spent and will not need to depend on the timer, although some kids like to watch the time count down.

- When the time out is over, remind the child why he was in time out (e.g., "You were in time out for hitting and we don't hit others") and ask him to make amends by apologizing to the person they hurt. A hug can be offered to younger kids, but the briefer and more matter-of-fact the interaction the better. We don't want kids getting into time out just to get affection from their parent at the end of the process.

Physical Punishment

Straus & Paschall (2009) followed children over the course of four years and determined that those who were spanked had lower IQs (up to 5 points) than their peers who were not spanked. Further, the more the children were spanked, the lower their IQs.

This debate is not new. In fact, I find myself in this debate at least a few times each month with some of the families I see. The age old question is whether or not spanking is an effective form of discipline. My professional stance (in conjunction with the research that supports it) is that spanking is actually punishment (not discipline) and is only "effective" in the short-term. Try telling that to the "old school" parent who swears, "It worked on me when my father spanked me!" With a little more investigation during history gathering with parents, I am often able to discern that while it may have garnered their attention as children in the short-term, it fueled resentment or fear toward the parents who were spanking them over the long-term, and potentially had a negative influence on the relationship. Some parents who use spanking with their child have asked me, "Why does my child not seem to be worried when he knows that he is going to get a spanking?" My response is, "Do you really want your child to fear you as means of getting your point across?"

I truly believe that the majority of spanking is in fact a form of a parental temper tantrum during which the parent has lost control and is at a loss for an effective discipline strategy. This is why having a pre-established parenting approach (strategies previously discussed in this chapter) is so important. Without a plan, there will be confusion, frustration, and a loss of patience that often leads to a loss of control (i.e., physical discipline). There are a number of problems with punishment that I encourage parents to consider when deciding if they really want to employ spanking as a method of punishment:

- Spanking focuses anger on the parent doing the spanking. When we resort to punishment it gives children someone else to be mad at or something else (the spanking) to blame.

- Spanking may cause the behavior to stop quickly, but in the absence of spanking, the negative behavior returns.

- Spanking does not teach accountability. The "punisher" (parent) is responsible to see that the child's behavior changes. The child learns nothing on their own as a result of the spanking.

- Punishment denies a child the right to experience the real consequence of their actions. If your child hurts someone else, for example, the other child may not want to play with your child anymore. Your child quickly forgets this possibility when spanking is introduced.

- A significant error occurs when we think that the punishment has taught the child what to do the next time a similar situation occurs. It has taught the child NOT to do something... but it has not taught them what they *should* do!

- The most important reason to not spank a child is that it models poor interacting. Spanking models for the child that physical aggression is how we get our point across. Especially when trying to curb a child's behavior of hitting, addressing this via spanking seems to be contrary to this goal. In other words, how is a child's hitting corrected by hitting them on the bottom?

In case those reasons were not enough, research indicates that spanking makes children anxious (especially toward the parent who is executing this method) and can lower self-esteem (Straus, 1994). A report endorsed by the American Academy of Pediatrics (Gershoff, 2008) looked at 100 years of research on spanking and concluded, "There is substantial research evidence that physical punishment makes it more, not less, likely that children will be defiant and aggressive in the future."

As stated previously, spanking often occurs when parents are at a loss for how to respond more effectively to their child's behavior. I know when I meet a parent who acknowledges spanking their child that they either don't have a plan or the one they have is not working. Hopefully the strategies outlined in this chapter will help to aid in the development of an effective approach. If you need more assistance, then you are encouraged to consult with a child psychologist to develop an effective plan based on your child's unique needs. Parents who are not quite ready to scrutinize themselves in a therapist's office are strongly encouraged to read books such as *1-2-3 Magic* (Phelan, 2003) that provide strategies designed to avoid the "talk-persuade-argue-yell-hit" syndrome of frustrated and exasperated parenting.

Establish Household Rules

One of the most effective ways to minimize conflict from occurring in the home is to establish a set of rules in your household before bad behavior occurs. These rules should be simple and clearly stated so that everyone understands them. The rules should be followed by the parent and child alike. I tell families to limit themselves to between three to five household rules. This way everyone can easily keep track of them and behave or respond to behaviors accordingly. Write them down and post them in a high traffic area of the home, if necessary, as a reminder.

I encourage rules emphasizing the values of safety, honesty, and respect. In fact, those are my own household rules: Safety, Honesty, and Respect. There may be subtexts under each heading. For example, the rule of respect may include speaking respectfully and respecting the personal space and possessions of other family members. I encourage establishing a personal area (likely the child's room) for each child in the home to store their personal possessions. This is an area in which siblings must ask to enter, and where toys and other valued items can be securely stored and are off limits. Anyone other than the owner (and parents) who enters this space without permission or consent will have consequences. However, if the child brings personal items into the general area and someone else decides to play with that item, these items become fair game and others can play with them on a first come, first served basis. If the items are left in a general living area of the home and are not cleaned up at the end of the day, I recommend the parent complete the labor and put each item that was not picked up into a laundry basket or other "toy time out bin" for at least 24 hours to signal to the child the importance of picking up after oneself. Do not say anything to the child until they ask where their favorite toy is. You then inform them it is in time out. This is a great way of teaching responsibility and executing a household rule without much interference. Just be sure that the child does not have access to the time out toy area so that you control when the time out is over and the toys are returned.

I recommend that parents sit down together and determine how they will respond to behaviors, especially for kids younger than thirteen. For example, parents may determine, "If my child is aggressive or destructive or unsafe, then [consequence] will occur." I encourage you to discuss your plan regarding the consequence that will be applied to a particular behavior and the reason why this will be the consequence (e.g., "Hitting is dangerous and hurts others so you will have an immediate time out when you hit") in advance with the child so that there is no argument at the time that a consequence is being administered. This allows the child fair notice of what the expectations are in the home, and also ensures that parents are consistent. The child may occasionally behave in ways you were not expecting. Don't panic. Try to determine the category of the behavior. Stay focused on how you decided you would respond and stick to that each and every time your child behaves that way. For example, you decided to use time out for hitting but the child spits at you. You view this as an aggressive and unacceptable action and thus it fits in the category of physical aggression, such as hitting. Thus, you use time out as a consequence just as you would if the child had hit you. Parents report feeling more confident and connected when they have a plan and execute it accordingly.

It can also be helpful to discuss parenting strategies with other family members, especially if they are actively involved with the child. Indeed, I often encourage extended family members who have regular contact with a child to attend my counseling sessions with the child and his immediate family provided that the parents are comfortable with this. Educating all participants in the child's life (including teachers and classmates, as deemed appropriate) can be extremely helpful to the child's progress. This approach is especially useful if the child spends any time away from their parents and in the homes of those extended family members, even for holiday visits or overnights. Whenever possible, having family members who have contact with this child be consistent in their approach with the child is critical.

This can be difficult for grandparents who want their grandchild to enjoy their visit and don't want to discipline the child. However, if the child is misbehaving throughout the visit, then grandma and grandpa will not be able to fully enjoy the visit with the child despite their unconditional love for the child. My suggestion is to address these behaviors immediately and in a firm, matter-of-fact manner so that the child understands that despite being in a different environment, the rules and expectations remain the same. Establishing a clear set of consequences for specific behaviors across home environments is essential.

Depending on the severity of the behavioral issue, I may advise families to regulate the behavior in the immediate home environment prior to allowing the child any extended visits with other family members. This is stressful for family members who want to see the child, but the alternative is that they see the child misbehave in their home as well, which is potentially more stressful for all involved. This also applies to taking the child out in public. Although the importance of taking the child out and about is stressed throughout this book, the reality is that you will not be successful unless the child is in control of most of his behaviors and is well-regulated. Thus, taking the child to a restaurant, for example, before he is able to sit through a meal at home for even five minutes will not be a productive exercise. Instead, devote your time and efforts rewarding the child for increasing amounts of time spent at the kitchen table during meals and once the child can sit successfully for 20 minutes, a restaurant experience may be indicated. You may need to start with a brief trip, such as ordering an appetizer only and then paying the check to begin to desensitize the child. Proceed at a comfortable pace that builds on previous successes.

Boundaries

The issue of boundaries comes up in a variety of situations. Most often, this involves difficulty related to physical or personal boundaries. Children with boundary difficulties tend to be "space invaders." For example, they may give hugs at inappropriate times or to inappropriate people, such as strangers or new acquaintances.

When I'm discussing this issue with children I will, depending on their age, try to use visuals to help explain physical space. For younger kids, it is useful to illustrate a comfortable distance between two people by extending your arms straight out to measure one arm's length. This is accomplished by having the child extend his arms like a mummy or zombie to get a sense of how far they should be standing from others. You can also lay a hula hoop on the floor and stand in the middle. Tell the child to stand outside the hula hoop as you have a discussion with him. He can walk around the hoop but cannot go inside of it. After he practices this enough, he will begin to acquire a sense of the space and won't have to put his arms out while talking to others. Another silly, yet effective, approach (depending on the sense of humor of the child) is the "taste of your own medicine" or "stick to you like glue" exercise. This involves staying as physically close as possible to the child, in a playful manner, as they walk around the room to give them a sense of how this feels when they invade the personal space of someone else.

Older kids can understand that the average comfortable distance between two people in American culture is approximately three feet. Another way to visually demonstrate distance and personal space is to get a roll of masking tape and make two boxes on the floor or create two "x's" (placed about 2-3 feet apart on the floor) as a demonstration where each person should stand during a conversation. Once the child seems to understand the physical boundaries, you can remove the "x's" and continue to practice.

Demands, Structure, and Predictability

Life is full of changes. These may be small changes (e.g., chicken for dinner instead of steak) or big changes (e.g., moving to a different state). Kids can experience adjustment-related difficulties in response to seemingly minor and temporary changes in routine like having a substitute teacher. In reference to school, many parents acknowledge increased stress experienced by the child following long, extended breaks from school, such as returning to school after the holidays. The same can be true when transitions from school to home occur--as in the end of the school year. Although summer tends to be rewarding and relaxing, the anticipation itself can fuel anxiety about the unknown and the lack of structure.

I offer the following general suggestions to sustain happiness and sanity throughout summer and school breaks:

- Increase predictability at home. This involves scheduling the days, although flexibility should be allowed. For example, one rule may be "Awake by 10 a.m. because we have to go to camp." But, there is no need to be overly scheduled for no apparent reason (e.g., "Be up by 9 a.m. because I said so"). The more children know what to expect, the less stress will occur when making transitions.
- Schedule a portion of each day, then allow the child to have input regarding the remainder of the day's activities. You may need to offer a list of suggestions for him to choose from, but you should not be trying to win the contest for "Entertainer of the Year." It

is not your responsibility to ensure that your child is having fun all the time!

- It may be useful to have a written or picture schedule for some children. This is especially helpful if, for example, the child is having resting time in the afternoon and comes to you to say, "*I'm booooored!*" You can calmly remind him that this is resting time, refer them to the schedule, and add "I know you will figure out something to do."

- Children generally have fewer demands on them during breaks, which is why they often do better behaviorally. Parents need breaks too! If you need breaks as a parent, then don't over schedule. Your kids will pick up on your stress and react accordingly.

- Remember to limit television time. The recommendation for television viewing is 1-2 hours each day (which includes screen time such as computers and video games). Some children can effectively manage more, others cannot. Certainly, exceptions can be made for special treat movie night, family videos, etc. It is always a good idea to monitor the time being spent viewing screens because school will again be in session and the child will have to "detox" as they try to refocus on schoolwork. Maybe reading a fun book together in exchange for some of that TV time (e.g., library summer reading program for prizes) can help keep the brain cells fresh and sharp?

- Whenever possible, prepare the child in advance for extended breaks and changes in routine. It never hurts to discuss what will take place (as much as you can anticipate *before* the first family argument occurs), and how long the break will last.

There are other times of the year when behaviors can amplify as well. This is especially obvious during the winter months, when kids have snow days. One would think that being off school is relaxing for a child, and in many instances it is. However, if the child lives in a state like Michigan where it snows a *lot* in the winter, this becomes very disruptive to the rhythm and flow of the school year. Indeed, many children I counsel do well in school during the fall when they are able to get into a rhythm and the only interruptions are Thanksgiving and then the holiday break. Kids return to school after about two weeks off and the weather might only allow a day or two of their school routine before another snow day. This is also difficult for parents because it is nearly impossible to prepare ahead of time for a snow day, especially given the difficulties meteorologists seem to have making an accurate weather prediction in the winter! Thus, although life is unpredictable and kids do need to learn to adjust, it is our job as parents to consider increasing the structure of the day during these times.

During times of adjustment, then, it is essential to keep the demands that we place on children reasonable and realistic. Some kids can keep up with consistent demands throughout the school year, but for the child who is reacting strongly during transitional periods, we need to consider altering the demands. If the child is in school, it is recommended that workloads be kept low during transitional periods so that the child can regulate his stress and reintegrate. I am not saying that the child should get away with doing nothing, but that we give him space to rebuild confidence and ensure success. Perhaps we increase the amount of small breaks throughout each school day during these periods of time. We can increase the expectations and demands *gradually* over time as the adjustment period ends.

Monitor/Feedback Loop

Behavior modification is not only about what parents, teachers, or therapists need to do in order to alter or manage a child's behavior. There must be a balance between how much adults prompt the child and provide redirection, and how much the child monitors and regulates his own behavior. Children with social skills difficulties often have a difficult time paying attention to their own behaviors and how those behaviors affect others around them. Beyond monitoring, there is a need for the child to learn about the *feedback loop*. This teaches him how his behavior affects others and how that effect comes full circle. For example, if a child hums in class it may bother the other students who are trying to work. If it continues, the other students may become annoyed with the child who hums and may sit apart from him or avoid him altogether. Thus, humming in class affects not only the classroom environment, but also how the other students view the child and interact with him.

You will recall from this chapter that "space invaders" refers to children that struggle with personal space. These children must learn to pay attention to how close they stand to others and the rules surrounding physical contact with others (e.g., good touch, bad touch). Other behaviors that require monitoring are perseverative behaviors. These behaviors are often characterized as "repetitive" or "relentless" by parents and can include opening and closing doors, turning switches on and off, but can also be anything the child discusses or requests over and over (e.g., "Can we go to the store? Can we go to the store?" and on and on). The goal is to reach a point in which the child self-imposes or at least recognizes a limit on how much they play with a particular object, discuss a particular topic of interest, or repeat a question or request.

I liken this behavior to a "brain hiccup," and children either feel helpless while attempting to stop the behavior or may lack the awareness that they are engaging in the behavior at all. Until a child learns how to recognize the behavior and stop it, it is the role of the parents or other adults who have consistent contact with the child to limit, point out, and perhaps eventually stop the child's participation in these activities, depending on the appropriateness or purpose.

A reasonable guideline is to limit any perseverative interests or behaviors to 20-30 minutes per day. This is useful because you can tell the child, "I know you really want to play Star Wars, but remember that we only do that for 20 minutes after dinner." You may even "prescribe" the behavior and set aside a block of time each day that the child is instructed to engage in the behavior. If trying to stop the behavior, then have the prescribed time take place during a time in which the child could be engaging in another enjoyable activity such as television or a special treat, like dessert. Thus, if the behavior is that important then the child would want to engage in it no matter what he is missing.

Once you have some time limits set on the behaviors, consider using the perseverative behavior as a means of engaging with your child and begin to steer the behavior into a social interest. The child who reads alone for long period of time, for example, may benefit from joining a library or community book club to discuss books with others. If this is too big a leap, then the baby step might be to read a book with your child and practice discussing it before joining a group of unfamiliar kids. A child who engages in fantasy pretend play in his room alone after school is likely trying to cope with the stress of the day. Perhaps he would allow you, despite his initial resistance, to be part of the fantasy or role-play. As a parent, it is essential that you remember to keep your focus on the *process.* In this case, your child is allowing you to play *with* him and the play is now social because it involves another person. I can't tell you how many parents miss some golden opportunities with their kids because they are hung up on the *content* of the play (e.g., "I don't think it's appropriate for my 12-year-old to play with puppets!"). Beggars can't be choosers, it is important to begin somewhere.

In other words, I don't think it matters (when first starting out) what the theme of the play is or whether the child is playing games that "much younger kids play" (as is often the complaint of parents). The focus should be on how the interest can be turned into something that involves other people and is not so object-oriented or solitary in nature. Take the opportunity to join the child in the game and use that time to help the child bring the play into a more developmentally appropriate range of content. If the child is insistent on playing with items that the peer group would criticize for being "babyish" or inappropriate (e.g., a comfort blanket for an 11-year-old boy), then discuss with the child the importance of keeping these items or topics of discussion reserved for private times at home, and teach him how to join in some of his peers' interests while at school.

Motivating a child to self-monitor can be difficult. Self-monitoring refers to the process whereby a child pays attention to a particular behavior they engage in (what it is, when it happens, for how long), and the effect it has on others. As discussed above, children may engage in perseverative behaviors as a means of regulating themselves or relieving stress or anxiety. Some kids may even take offense initially at the idea of being asked to decrease or stop engaging in a behavior that they perceive to be useful to their daily functioning, despite its disruption to the lives of others. These children will need to be offered alternatives, such as less disruptive behaviors, to achieve the same desired outcome after changing the behavior. With the example of the child who hums while completing work (and annoys the rest of the class), perhaps the humming helps to maintain concentration. If squeezing a stress ball can accomplish the same goal, then replacing humming by offering the child a stress ball can help both the child and his peers.

Difficulty with self-monitoring, for the child who is motivated to change his behavior, is not necessarily due to lack of desire, but rather forgetfulness. Enter technology. One of my favorite features of the Sōsh mobile app is *Monitor*, which allows the parent, teacher, therapist, or child to set a random or fixed time interval in which the device (e.g., iPod Touch, iPad 2, or iPhone) will beep. The point is that each time the device beeps (which is designed to be very quick and not disruptive to the environment), the child is instructed to pay attention to what they are doing. So if it beeps and the child is looking out the window, the beep should alert the child to redirect focus. The nice thing about this is that it encourages the child to be an active participant and keeps adults from having to do all the work. Also, capturing video of the child engaging in the behavior he needs to self-monitor helps him to become more self-aware, especially if he can review the video and track behaviors, such as how frequently and how long he hums over the course of a five minute video clip of him working on an assignment in class.

Interest Log

Consistent with the *Monitor* timer feature of the Sōsh app, I encourage children and their families to track strong or dominating interests as a means of increasing awareness of how long the child spends on these interests (you can use the *Interest Log* on the Sōsh mobile app), and what effect it has on others. If your interest log reflects five hours of

Star Wars each weekend day, but other kids in school are really into music, then it may be important to broaden interests as a means of making connections with others. A little Star Wars is fine, but you know the saying, "variety is the spice of life," and too much of anything (or any *one* thing) is less than ideal. Further, taking note of how much time is spent alone participating in the things on your *Interest Log* may help to encourage more outings. The goal is to find balance--not necessarily cutting out activities, but instead participating in at least one thing that involves others, especially if the interest log reflects only solitary activities. If a child has five hours to watch or think about Star Wars each day, for example, then he doesn't have much time for people or interactions. Without activities involving other people, a child will not be able to improve his social skills.

Voice Meter

Some children with social difficulties may experience difficulty regulating the volume of their speech. Although a qualified speech pathologist is the ideal treatment provider to help a child with such an issue, it can be useful to provide the child with his own tool to monitor volume. Before developing the Sōsh app, I utilized a color-coded visual scale with kids in treatment, and I had to point to where their voice volume was (red = too loud, green = just right). Kids would often disagree with my rating or accuse me of being "mean" because of the feedback. The *Voice Meter* on the Sōsh app assists the child in learning how to regulate his vocal volume. If you are not using the Sōsh app, then a visual graph or color scale may be of some use to the child, although this requires another person be available to point out on the scale how loud the child is talking, and opens up an opportunity for a child to disagree with the ratings.

Key Points

- The ability to **Regulate** is to adjust, control, and manage your behaviors. It is also the ability to calm yourself when excited or dysregulated, or when feedback from others suggests that you should alter your behavior in some way.

- Behavior does *not* explain causes. What might appear to be an attention problem, distractibility, or oppositional defiance may be related to a learning difficulty, autism spectrum diagnosis, depression, anxiety, etc. Without a thorough and appropriate clinical assessment it is difficult to determine what is motivating the behavior.

- One of the most effective ways to minimize conflict from occurring in the home is to establish a set of rules in your household before "bad" behavior occurs. These rules should be simple and clearly stated so that everyone understands them.

- Rewards can be given immediately after a behavior that you would like to see increase.

- Ignoring can be an effective tool to decrease the incidence of a behavior. Effective ignoring means no looking, no talking, and no touching.

- Time Out is a time away from any attention from others. This technique is generally reserved for dangerous, destructive, or aggressive behaviors.

- Physical punishment is not effective and is usually a parent's response to feeling frustrated with a behavior.

Chapter Seven

Recognize: Understand Feelings

Recognize: Understand Feelings

Brian is experiencing difficulties with regard to his social interactions with peers. Teachers describe his behaviors as "impulsive." He routinely blurts out answers to questions without raising his hand. Brian tells his family that he is "different" from other kids and he is upset about this, often to the point of tearfulness. While attending school and while completing school work at home, it seems he *wants* to pay more attention to what he is doing, but his brain does not allow it. His peers often tell him that he is "immature" and implore him to "grow up." In school, he is below grade level in multiple developmental areas. Brian, now 13 years old, is enticed by the suggestions of his peers to make inappropriate gestures in front of the classroom teacher. Despite his age, Brian does not yet understand that these gestures may elicit laughter and cheers when performed exclusively among peers, but that engaging in these behaviors in front of teachers is inappropriate and will result in negative consequences.

Socially, Brian does not have good comprehension of humor. He does understand that he is supposed to laugh after someone tells a joke, but has difficulty understanding *why* the joke was funny. He often misses social cues and the subtleties of social interactions. These are interpreted literally, which results in him appearing awkward to his peers. Brian was recently told to "take a hike" by a group of kids to which he replied in a matter-of-fact tone, "I don't like walking that much." He wants to be accepted by his peers and therefore tends to be a follower. He can be quite sensitive, as evidenced by repeated tearful outbursts, and he has significant difficulty understanding basic social norms. For example, he may argue with a peer at school who is attempting to use a piece of gym equipment that Brian recently played with but is not currently using. Brian believes his previous use of the equipment gives him "ownership" of it. His peers are dumbfounded in response to these behaviors and his parents report that other children find him to be somewhat "odd" or "weird."

The term **Recognize** suggests identifying something familiar. When walking in a store, if we see a person who looks familiar, we say that we "recognize" them. The term **Recognize** in Sōsh refers to the ability to perceive, to acknowledge, and to accurately identify feelings that you and others experience.

Note: Many of the strategies presented in this chapter are designed to be modified for home, school, and other environments where adults may be trying to help a child increase social skills and emotional awareness. Thus, creative and personalized modifications of the following approaches are encouraged.

Daily Check-In

A highly recommended strategy to help in the **Recognize** domain is a daily check-in with the child, focusing on emotions and feelings. Whether the child is at home or in school, he is encouraged to practice connecting emotions with thoughts and actions. This can be with an adult (i.e., teacher, parent, therapist, counselor), as well as with one or more peers. The child is instructed to identify recent thoughts or actions and connect each of these to feeling happy, sad, mad, or worried. Thus, the child is asked, "Tell me about a thought or situation that made you feel happy today" and then the question is repeated for sad, mad, and worried (or replace with scared, nervous, or anxious). Each of these areas can be explored further at the adult's discretion, and depending on the child's willingness to elaborate.

Another part of the check-in process is the identification of a challenge, in which a child creates a personal goal to attain for that day. It is ideal to complete the check-in and challenge process early in the day so the child has an idea of how they are feeling to start out his day and what he wants to work on as the day goes on. It may be helpful to complete a second check-in later in the day, so the child has time to gather information about what went well and what didn't go well and how those experiences relate to the challenge. As with all of these strategies, you can adjust them and their timing to suit your specific needs.

A thorough explanation of the check-in process and the reasons for it (e.g., it will help him understand how feelings and thoughts are linked, which will help him socially) should be given to the child before implementation. In particular, the adult explains the process of identifying thoughts, feelings, and behaviors by giving everyday examples of such connections. For example, the adult may talk about how, after hitting a baseball (behavior), he often thinks to himself that he is a good baseball player (thought) and feels happy (feeling).

Purpose and Content

A check-in serves a number of purposes for the child and adult alike. First, check-ins allow the adult to gauge the child's emotional functioning. For example, a child may report, "I feel sad that I argued with my sister today," or "I'm happy that I got invited to a birthday party." These disclosures can then provide topics for discussion. Second, the check-in provides the child with the opportunity to identify and accurately label his emotional status. This is especially important for individuals with social skills difficulty because many of these individuals have trouble expressing their emotions verbally and also struggle to link emotions with logic (e.g., "I know that I should not tell her that her haircut looked ugly, but I don't understand why she has to get so upset about it. I was just being honest!").

As children become more acquainted with the check-in process, some may repeat the same thought or behavior connected to feeling sad, mad, happy, or worried. These children are using repetition to escape the check-in process and should be asked to formulate alternative examples of their feelings. A child's overuse of a particular theme allows for regurgitation of "safe" information and discourages deeper exploration of emotion. In some cases, a "no-repeat" list may be constructed, which identifies certain examples no longer permitted to be reported as a primary feeling. For instance, a child may indicate he felt sad about losing while playing a video game. The child may then begin providing this example daily as something he is sad about in an effort to avoid active participation in the check-in exercise. The "no-repeat" list would then identify "playing video games" under the sad category as being an inappropriate example of the primary feeling of being sad.

Challenges

Another important task for children to complete once they have connected their feelings to events is the identification of a daily personal challenge. As stated above, a challenge is a cognitive or behavioral goal a child wants to achieve that has been difficult to accomplish in the past. Challenges should be based on four key factors. They must be: 1) Attainable, 2) Positive, 3) Observable, and 4) Immediate. For example, a personal challenge might be to start a conversation with one person today. Adults can model examples of a challenge to help children define their goals. It may also be useful to recount recent situations in which the child struggled and ask how he could behave differently in the future. It is important to ask the child how he will know if the challenge has been accomplished. This helps to define the thoughts or actions necessary for successful completion of the challenge. If the child is using the Sōsh mobile app, then he can enter these challenges or goals for himself into the app, which is set up to guide the development of goals based on the above four factors.

A useful challenge must have several characteristics. First, it must be **attainable**. Kids who never reach their challenges are unlikely to be interested in setting new ones. So, creating realistic challenges will aid in progress. For example, a child who says he wants to play with every person in his class during a particular day is setting up an unrealistic challenge. One way in which the adult can help reformulate such a challenge is to set the goal that the child will play with, say, at least one classmate today. If he ends up playing with more than one classmate, even better! Creating attainable goals increases the potential for success and improved self-esteem.

The second characteristic of an appropriate challenge is that it must be **positively** stated. Children have a tendency to formulate challenges in terms of what they will not do (e.g., "*not* get into trouble"). The goal is to restate their challenges in positive terms. The preceding example, if phrased positively, would state, "I will follow classroom rules today." The idea is for the child to become more adept at identifying what he will do as opposed to what he should not be doing.

The third requirement is that the challenge must be **measurable**. For example, a commonly voiced challenge is, "Have a good day." Obviously, this is difficult to measure, due to the subjectivity of "good." What specifically is the child hoping goes well? If he is interested in academic success, the challenge might be to get at least 8 out of 10 words correct on his spelling test. This permits the child's progress toward meeting the challenge to be measured.

The final requirement in formulating a useful challenge during check-in is that the challenge must be **immediate**. The adult should encourage the child to formulate a challenge that can be attempted on that particular day, and in the environment in which it was intended. If the check-in process is taking place in school, the challenge "Ignore my older sister when she tries to get me in trouble in the backyard" is not ideal. Instead, the child is encouraged to challenge himself with something related to school where he can be observed and can receive feedback from adults, and have access to the individual(s) or activity he is incorporating into the challenge.

Active/Reflective Listening

Perhaps one of the best references on the topic of improving communication between parents and kids is the book *How to Talk so Kids Will Listen and Listen so Kids will Talk* (Faber & Mazlish, 1999). If you don't have time to read the book, be aware that kids will often surprise you with the comments they make. Before jumping in with advice or even discipline, it's almost always more important to listen first. As a parent, put yourself in the proper frame of mind: "I'm going to hear him out and find out exactly what he thinks and how he feels about what's going on." Next, several strategies can be utilized to help expand the conversation with your child. These include openers, nonjudgmental questions, reflecting feelings, and perception checks (Phelan, 2003). These strategies become especially important when trying to communicate with your child during the 'tween and teen years.

Openers

Begin with brief comments or questions designed to elicit further information from your child. These comments may appear overly passive, but remember that active listening must precede any problem-solving discussion. If discipline or other action is necessary, worry about that after you have obtained all of the facts. Openers can be simple: "Oh?" or "Wow!" for example. Be flexible with your response as long as it communicates that you are ready and willing to listen sympathetically. Nonverbal behavior, such as sitting down beside the child (to avoid any anxiety that may result from a face-to-face discussion) or putting down the cell phone or newspaper to look at him is also very helpful.

Nonjudgmental Questions

Following openers, more questions are often necessary. To be effective, these must not be "loaded" or judgmental. "What do you think made you do that?" or "It sounds like this is really bothering you" tend to work well. Avoid questions such as, "What were you thinking?" or "What's your problem today?" Of course, tone of voice is critical here. The more you come across to the child as abrasive or harsh, the more likely he is to shut down and stop communicating.

Reflecting Feelings

If you are going to tell someone that you think you understand him, try to let him know that you can imagine how he must have felt (or is presently feeling) under the circumstances. For example, "Boy, I haven't seen you this mad in a while!" or "That must have been very hard for you." Reflecting feelings lets the child know that whatever he is feeling is fine, it's what he sometimes *does* about it or how he *behaves* at the time that may be the problem. Reflecting feelings reinforces self-esteem and also helps diffuse negative feelings so they are not acted out somewhere else. A child who tells you, "You don't love me!" might benefit from a response that reflects his feelings rather than one that attempts to convince him that he does not really feel that way. One possible response could be, "I can see that you are really upset right now."

Perception Checks

From time to time, it is helpful to determine whether or not you have a good understanding of what the child is saying. This type of comment not only lets you know whether you understand him correctly, it also has a second purpose: it tells the child that you are really listening and trying to see things from his perspective. "It sounds like you are pretty upset that the teacher had some trick questions on the test. Am I right about that?" or, "I could be wrong, but I have not seen you this mad in a long time!"

Active listening is essential for all parents. It involves sincerely trying to understand what someone else is thinking even if you don't agree. It's also a great self-esteem builder, and you will find if you listen well you can learn a lot about what your children think about life. In fact, you can often obtain more information from your child by listening and making comments about what they are saying than by interrogating them. Give it a try. It takes practice, but soon you will be learning more about your child's day than you initially thought possible.

Video Feedback

Kids who struggle recognizing their own emotions and nuances of social interactions, and those of others, can benefit from the use of video feedback (Boles & Bowers, 2003). Video cameras are a great way to give kids feedback on their interaction style. I encourage parents to be creative and use video taping in their everyday interactions with the child at home, and schools to request consent to use video taping in their daily interactions with the children. The wonderful thing about technology such as iPod Touch (4th gen.), iPhone, and iPad 2 is that you can record video with these devices. The Sōsh app provides a list of activities that incorporate video and audio recording so that kids know what to work on and how to do it while also having instant access to the video or audio for review and practice. For example, one exercise could be for the child to video record a conversation with a peer (with their knowledge and consent), and then review it to monitor the child's tone of voice or inflection and the amount of affect used, or to look for nonverbal indicators (i.e. smiling or other facial expressions of emotion).

Several psychotherapy treatment concepts have been effectively administered utilizing video strategies. For instance, students learn to express and recognize feelings using video cameras. This is a fairly easy exercise. An adult can construct a list of feelings and instruct the child to stand in front of the camera and provide an example of how he exhibits that particular feeling. The feelings can initially be modeled by the adult. So, for the feeling of sadness the adult might make a frown and begin to "cry." Once the feelings are modeled by the adult as needed, the child can take the lead and the adult can record him.

Next, the videotape is reviewed in an effort to help the child become more adept at recognizing his own (and other people's) feelings based on visual cues. The use of close-up shots helps to identify and study nonverbal expressions such as facial movements, eye contact, etc. The adult should remain very active during the video review process, pausing the video and encouraging discussion and interpretation when warranted. As always, any rewards distributed to the child (e.g., a piece of candy for each correct answer) while initially completing video reviews with the child can sustain interest in the activity and help make it a pleasurable experience rather than a chore.

Still Photography

Still photography has been utilized as an alternative approach to engage children in social skills work and reduce anger during difficult periods, such as time-outs or transitions. A digital camera is ideal due to its capacity to immediately create and delete photographs and view/print them on a computer. The child can again be involved in scripted situations in which target behaviors are observed. The adult will model appropriate snapshots and capture key behaviors, such as appropriate interactions or inappropriate physical aggression. The child is then asked to "pose" in these situations while being photographed. Next, have the child view the photograph on the digital display or on the computer monitor and ask the child what the next picture might look like if taken 30 seconds later. For example, the child might take a picture of a boy standing next to a group of other kids who are laughing, while the boy is looking sad. We can then ask the child to tell us why the boy looks sad, what the kids might be discussing, and how the boy might approach the group in order to be included. The primary goal is establishment of the connection between behaviors and consequences, which helps to improve social skills.

Another way in which still photography can be beneficial is by having the child take pictures of events in the classroom, or at home. This can include an assignment to have the child be a "reporter" for the classroom (provided that the necessary parental consents for photography have been obtained) so that during special events (e.g., Halloween, Valentine's party) or projects the child is responsible for taking pictures.

This gives the child a purpose and reason to interact with others, and also permits development of an admirable skill. Other kids typically enjoy having their picture taken, so they will tend to interact more with the reporter. The class can then work together to put a "yearbook" or other collection together at the end of the year or periodically (websites like *Shutterfly*, *Picaboo*, *Mypublisher*, and *Lulu* allow the creation of beautiful photo books). This encourages group cohesion and cooperation, and gives the child a useful and valuable role. If the child is able to use an Apple device with a built-in camera in school, then a separate digital camera is not necessary. Instructions should be provided concerning the nature of acceptable photographs (e.g., no inappropriate body language or pictures of people they do not have permission to photograph).

This empowerment to take their own pictures can be very useful in creating responsibility and encouraging active participation among peers. If the child uses a disposable camera, the adult should have the pictures developed so they can be reviewed and explained by the child to peers in a manner similar to show-and-tell. The Sōsh app has a feature built in so the child can simply open the Camera Roll on the device to immediately show the photos. The iPad 2 has an HDMI output that allows anything on the device to be viewed on a television, such as in a classroom. This activity is an excellent way to connect with the peer group and share some aspects of life outside of school that others may not get to see. Sometimes, a peer will compliment a child on one of his pictures, which may result in the child having a confidence boost and perhaps even an invitation to that peer to come over to play!

Feelings Posters

Still photographs of "feelings faces" may also provide students with the opportunity to identify feelings that correspond with facial expressions, and can serve as a reminder for commonly displayed emotions in the child's life. Kids often enjoy making feelings posters for their room that show their own faces expressing emotions, as opposed to the cartoon faces found on many commercial posters. The use of a handheld mirror is especially helpful while the child is attempting to "pose" his face in order to express a particular emotion. The mirror provides immediate feedback and allows the child to modify his expression accordingly. If you are using the Sōsh app, the front facing camera on the device allows the child time to "pose" his face and review the expression prior to taking the photo. Once he is confident that his facial expression accurately portrays the emotion to be identified, the photograph is taken. If you are not using the Sōsh app, the child can work with an adult to print the photos on a computer and arrange them on a poster board, making a personalized feelings poster for display and future reference. A feelings poster depicting four emotions (fully customizable by the user) is included within the Sōsh app for portability and quick reference.

Read, Watch, and Discuss

All of these particular skills (i.e., read, watch, discuss) develop over time, and the best way to develop them from an early age is to read a variety of books with your child and discuss them. This practice also helps to promote a child's social skills development. Children can read fairy tales and short stories and look for details that illustrate how the characters feel. Children can also compare and contrast characters in different stories. For example, how is the wicked stepmother in *Cinderella* different from the wicked witch in *Sleeping Beauty*? Children can search for examples that demonstrate the characters' wicked personalities. When working with fiction texts, encourage the child to draw upon prior knowledge and his own experiences to make connections with the characters as they read. As kids get older and their interests change, so too does the content of what they want to read. The activity, however, remains the same regarding the discussion of themes, feelings of the characters, etc.

I also recommend that a parent watch movies or sitcoms with the child or as a family activity. Try muting the television for selected portions of the show or movie, and try to guess what the characters are thinking and feeling based on their mannerisms and gestures. Mute the commercials and use that time to discuss what just happened. If you limit the child's screen time as a family rule, then you can agree that he can watch an extra show as long and he watches and discusses it with you. Whether it is with books or watching certain television shows, try to spend at least some time documenting the thoughts and feelings of the characters. Create your own log page, or use the *Feelings* feature of the Sōsh mobile application, shown below.

Triggers

Cognitive Behavioral Therapy (CBT) is based on the idea that our thoughts cause our feelings and behaviors, as opposed to external causes like people, situations, and events. The way to "dissect" the origin of your feelings is to first identify the situation in which these feelings began. Consider the child who feels sad during the lunch hour each day. The situation in this case is being in the lunch room. Perhaps we add that the child sits alone during each lunch period. The next variable is the thought. In this example, the child begins to think to himself, "I'm invisible. No one wants to sit with me." Next, we ask the child to identify the feeling that corresponds with those thoughts. The child responds, "I feel *sad* every time I go to lunch." Finally, we identify the behavior. In this case, the child sits alone while eating lunch. If he loses his appetite, plays with this food, or puts his head down on the table, these behaviors would be included as well. This continuum is often referred to as "S-T-E-B," which refers to Situations, Thoughts, Emotions, and Behaviors. The way to make yourself feel better, according to CBT, is to intervene at the thought stage. Thus, instead of the child thinking "I'm invisible. No one wants to sit with me," he might change his thinking to, "Sure, those kids don't want to talk to me, but it's because I don't know them that well. It's not because I am a bad person or unlikable." This type of thinking will decrease his likelihood of feeling sad, and point the way to constructive goal-setting in order to improve the situation.

The particular therapeutic techniques vary within the different approaches of CBT, but common strategies include keeping a diary of significant events and associated feelings, thoughts and behaviors; questioning and testing cognitions, assumptions, evaluations and beliefs that might be unhelpful and unrealistic; gradually facing activities which may have been avoided; and trying out new ways of behaving and reacting. The Sōsh application is designed to guide kids through all of these strategies. Relaxation, mindfulness, and distraction techniques are also commonly included as part of a CBT protocol (see **Relax** chapter). If you are interested in exploring these options more in-depth, I recommend that you consult with a psychologist who is skilled in Cognitive Behavioral Therapy (CBT).

I credit David Burns (1999) for bringing the principles of CBT into popular culture. He built on the work of Aaron Beck (cited in Beck, 1995) and noted that people who are at-risk for becoming sad or depressed often indulge in the following cognitive biases (Burns, 1999, pp. 40-41):

- **All-or-Nothing Thinking**: You place things into black and white categories, ignoring the exceptions and subtle shades of gray, "It's perfect or defective," "I'm lovable or unlovable," "I either succeeded or failed."

- **Overgeneralization**: A few bad experiences make you believe that all similar situations will turn out badly. You see a never-ending pattern, where exceptions cannot exist; "Since I've made several bad decisions, I'll always make bad decisions."

- **Labeling**: A form of overgeneralization, often in the form of name-calling: "I'm a loser," "I'm a failure," "I'm unlovable."

- **Discounting the Positives**: Positives are explained away, they "don't count." You minimize or entirely disqualify your resources, your ability to cope, possible help from others, alternative opportunities, etc.

- **Jumping to Conclusions:**
  - A. **Fortune Telling:** You constantly anticipate and predict future situations will turn out badly, often despite the absence of facts.
  - B. **Mind Reading:** You assume that you know why and what others are thinking, feeling and doing, without proof.

- **Magnification (Catastrophizing):** You focus on what might be lost and exaggerate either how likely it is to happen or how terrible it will be when it does: "I'll probably be rejected, and that's terrible," or "It's horrible that I lost."

- **Emotional Reasoning:** You reach conclusions based on your feelings, "I feel this way so it must be," "It feels terrible, so it must be terrible," "I'll wait until I feel like doing this."

- **Absolute Thinking:** A rigid and inflexible type of thinking. Sometimes takes the form of demanding (of yourself) that things should be what they are not. You think with over-simplistic phrases such as *"should's, must's, cant's, have-to's, ought's."* This is often a misguided attempt to increase motivation, which instead only produces procrastination, guilt and frustration; "I can't stand it," "I must do my best all the time," "I can't stand losing."

- **Mental Filter:** You find and then dwell on negatives and other losses. Information that confirms your negative views is seen as proof, while facts that don't fit are seen as rare exceptions and ignored; "Nothing good ever happens to me," "I will always lose," "No one cares about me."

- **Personalization:** You mistakenly believe you are the cause of events and that you're the reason people act and feel as they do; "I was rejected because of my looks or my job."

- **Blaming**: The opposite of personalization. The reason bad things are happening is because of what the other person is doing or not doing. You overlook your own contributions to the problem.

Children with social difficulties may benefit from using aspects of this theory in their everyday interactions. Ask the child to reflect on events, situations, or "things" that upset him and then identify what helps in that situation, as well as what is not helpful. Too often these kids are stuck and repeat the same dysfunctional approach to a situation despite the lack of previous success.

Shades of Gray/False Dilemma

The notion of Shades of Gray comes from my experience working with kids who tend to see the world and their everyday interactions in terms of black-and-white or all-or-nothing. This type of logical fallacy is often referred to as a "false dilemma." Simply stated, it occurs when *only* two mutually exclusive alternatives are considered, when in fact there are additional options. An example is, "Either he's a fraud or he's truly psychic."

False dilemmas can arise intentionally, when fallacy is used in an attempt to force a choice (e.g., "If it doesn't fit, you must acquit"). A fallacy can also arise by accidental omission of additional options rather than by deliberate deception (e.g., "I thought we were friends, but all my friends were at my party over the weekend and you were not there"). This type of reasoning is dangerous and often the by-product of mental inflexibility, which was addressed in the **Reason** chapter.

The idea is to help children see the world in shades of gray rather than just in black and white. Arguing with a mentally inflexible child over his singular thinking rarely results in positive outcomes. Instead, offering tools to increase flexibility can assist in broadening alternatives. Whenever possible, talk to the child about his style of thinking and how it affects others. Then take it one step further and tell the child how his behavior ultimately affects the way others see him. For example, consider the child who thinks that the way other kids play soccer on the playground is "unfair" and he points this out on a daily basis. We can sit down with the child and explain that we understand his desire to keep all things fair, but that this recurrent pattern of accusing others of behaving unfairly is not helpful. We can point out how this repetitive accusation causes the other kids to become upset with the child. Further, if the other kids are upset with him, it lessens the chances that they will want to continue to play with him, or perhaps want to be his friend.

If this type of discussion does not seem to "sink in" with the child (after repeated trials), or if the child is defensive about the situation, you may want to consider finding children's books about the specific problem so that the child can begin to look at it from outside of himself, using a "third party" perspective. You can also write stories about the situation with the child and replace the human characters with animals, as in a fable. Finally, the use of actions figures, dolls, or puppets to act out difficult scenarios may help deliver the message, depending on the developmental level or interests of the child.

For the more insightful or older child, consider the following exercise: To begin, make a list of commonly used opposites on a piece of paper. Next, write down a single word that accurately describes the middle ground between each pair of opposites. For example, if the words are hot and cold, good middle ground or shades of gray words would be "warm" or "lukewarm." The following list includes a number of sample opposites. Try the exercise yourself, being careful to avoid reading ahead until the activity is completed.

1.   Black and White

2.   Large and Small

3.   Up and Down

4.   Left and Right

5.   Fast and Slow

6.   Night and Day

7.   Light and Dark

8.   Tall and Short

9.   Easy and Hard

10.   Young and Old

11.   Big and Small

12.   Loud and Quiet

13.   Good and Bad

14.   Near and Far

15.   Pass and Fail

16.   Happy and Sad

17.   Clean and Dirty

18.   Light and Heavy

19.   Shy and Outgoing

20.   Calm and Anxious

Once you have finished your list of middle ground words, review all of the words you used. Do they have anything in common? If your list is anything like mine, all of the middle ground words are similar in at least one way: they're all a little boring and bland. Consider some possible answers. Obviously, the color "gray" falls between black and white, and I am guessing you wrote that one down. After all, that is the basis of this entire section. And where are you if you're not left or right? Well, you're "moderate" or in the "center." If you're not young or old, perhaps you're "middle-aged." What if you're buying a shirt and it's not small or large? It's probably a medium. *Middle-aged, moderate, average, gray.* Maybe you even wrote the words "normal," "so-so," or "average" on your paper.

Did you have trouble answering as you approached the end of the activity? If so, you are not alone. I could not find any way to accurately describe the middle ground between "shy and outgoing" or "calm and anxious" with a single word or even with a group of words. There's no convenient word or phrase in the English language, it seems, to describe the middle ground between some of the polar opposites listed above. How does this apparent deficiency of the English language harm us?

Take a look at the word list again. How often do you use words like "happy" and "sad?" You've probably uttered them today without even realizing it. After all, simplifying our stories for others with polar words like "sad" is convenient. It's easier for a college student to lament that his research paper is "going to take *forever*" to be completed (especially if he is seeking empathy) than to get into the details of exactly how much is completed and how much is left to write. And we're all guilty of watching a movie or reading the news and calling someone "the bad guy." After all, this sounds a lot more decisive than qualifying your statement and balancing it with a list of their positive attributes. Resorting to polar opposite words (in cases where a middle ground word would more accurately describe the situation) can change the "truth" of the situation that we are describing.

Each of the above pairs of opposites are examples of dichotomous thinking that, when applied to everyday life, can have negative effects on the way we see ourselves and others, or the situations that we encounter. Here's a classic example: "I think I totally failed my math test." The word "fail" falls at the polar end of the pass/fail continuum. If you find yourself saying or thinking something similar, stop. Step "out of your brain" for a second and engage in some meta-cognition, or thinking about the way that you are thinking (recall **Reason** chapter). How did you come to the conclusion that you *failed*? Use some CBT-oriented questions. Maybe you didn't ace the test, but are you *sure* that you failed? Is it possible that your performance may have fallen somewhere in the middle of "I aced it" and "I failed"?

Luckily, in school, there are letter grades from A through F that can extend the options along a continuum and help avoid dichotomous or black-and-white thinking. But in other contexts, it's not so easy. Let's say you tell a friend that you're feeling anxious. Perhaps you're certain that you're not calm, but how far from calm are you? Are you truly anxious with a racing heart, rapid breathing and sweaty palms, or are you somewhere in the middle of calm and anxious?

How can you decrease your black-and-white thinking, and how can your child do so? The answer is pretty simple: practice adding shades of gray into your everyday conversations and interactions. The Sōsh app provides several examples of commonly experienced emotional dichotomies and allows the user to scroll along a continuum to view the various shades of gray/feeling that occur between the opposite extremes. The user can then add personal black-and-white examples as well as the "betweens." The following list of questions may help your child become "unstuck" when he is using black-and-white logic (Beck, 1995, p. 109):

1. What is the evidence?

   What is the evidence that supports this idea?

   What is the evidence against this idea?

2. Is there an alternative explanation?

3. What is the *worst* that could happen? Could I live through it?

   What is the <u>best</u> that could happen?

   What is the most realistic outcome?

4. What is the effect when I believe my thought(s)?

   What could be the effect of changing my thinking?

5. What should I do about it?

6. What would I tell _____ (a friend, someone else) if

   he were in the same situation?

Further, you can begin to model appropriate "gray" language in your child's presence. Consider using the previous exercise to find "middle" or "gray" words with your child. In addition, if there is no good word to describe the middle ground, try using a number scale to describe the feeling. For example, with anxiety, if the absolute worst anxiety is a 10, then perhaps public speaking is a 7, thinking about a deadline at school is a 5, and playing outside is a 1 (note that "0" should not appear on this scale because no one is ever completely free from anxiety).

Try to catch yourself using this type of black-and-white thinking during the next few days. Make a note of the situations in which you use exaggerated words, then take a step back, assess your word choices, and improve your story with a "gray" word. You're turning 40 years old today and you just referred to yourself as "old." How true is this? Do you

know anyone who is older? Could you also be middle-aged? Isn't 40 the

new 30? How long do members of your family live? If the average life

expectancy in your family is 95, isn't 40 less than half of your life

expectancy (not to mention the advances in medical science over the next

50 years that could add further years to your life)? Sure, it's "old" when

you compare your current age with memories of your childhood, but

along the continuum of life, 40 is pretty much "in the middle."

Mindfulness

Several definitions of mindfulness have been used in modern

Western psychology. According to various prominent psychological

definitions, mindfulness refers to a psychological quality that involves

bringing one's complete attention to the present experience on a moment-

to-moment basis, or paying attention in a particular way: with purpose, in

the present moment, in which each thought, feeling, or sensation that

arises is acknowledged and accepted as it is (Bishop et al., 2004).

Mindfulness is important because it has been shown to reduce mood

difficulties and stress (Brown & Ryan, 2003). It is also one of the

fundamentals of meditation, although meditation is outside of the scope

of this book.

One way to begin to understand the concept of mindfulness is to

hold a piece of fruit, such as an orange, in your hand and study it. Focus

all of your attention on the orange: the way it feels, the weight, the shape,

the pores in its skin, the color, and even the smell. Other thoughts will

naturally begin to enter into your mind during this exercise. Your goal is

to stay focused on the orange in the moment, and let any competing

thoughts pass. This exercise demonstrates how much the human brain

wants to focus on many things at once. Our brains also dwell on the past (which can be upsetting depending on how we reflect on our history) and try to predict the future (which can make us anxious with "what if" questions). The only way to truly be "at peace" with ourselves is to remain in the moment and acknowledge things for what they are. All we know about the orange, in this example, is that we are holding it in our hand and it has a particular set of physical and sensory properties.

Mindfulness is a form of meditation that requires daily practice to do it well. However, it is often helpful to use it on an ad hoc basis if you don't have the time to do it daily. For example, I sometimes practice it after a long day at work while I am driving home. I work to keep my thoughts off the work day (the past) or what awaits me at home (the future), and focus instead on everything I experience "in the moment" during the drive home. This includes watching the speedometer go up and down, paying attention to billboards and other cars, but also involves turning the radio off so that I can focus in on the sounds of the car and the world around my vehicle. Within minutes, I begin to feel the stress and fatigue of the day dissipate.

Force a Smile/Hide Your Mouth

The force a smile exercise is useful if a child is having a bad day or is feeling "blue." Psychological research (Davis & Palladino, 2000) has demonstrated that the movement of the mouth muscles upward into the smile position (despite not having anything to smile about) releases endorphins into the body that help us feel better. Besides, it's difficult to be upset or angry if you are walking around with a smile on your face. This is also connected with the "behavior before mood" approach referenced in the **Relate** chapter (i.e., smiling is a behavior you can employ before you feel the corresponding emotion of happiness, and it may promote happiness).

I recommend that parents get into the habit of playfully engaging in a game of "force a smile" with their child to help ease the tension and burden associated with improving social skills. Also, it can be a nice way of reducing some anxiety as you approach transitions in your everyday life, or are preparing to begin a task or activity that may not be the child's first choice.

Although it often looks a little silly at first (which may be appealing to kids), using dust masks from a home improvement store can be a creative way to learn how to focus on subtle aspects of facial expressions in order to help understand feelings. The parent and the child take turns wearing the mask, which should cover your nose and mouth. Then, each person practices guessing the feelings of the person wearing the mask using only the visible portions of the face as clues. The person wearing the mask does not talk, but rather poses their face to demonstrate a particular emotion. With the lower portion of the face covered, the person guessing (usually the child) must begin to look for other cues to guess feelings. Perceived clues, such as how the eyes change or the wrinkle lines on the face, become more important to the overall emotional picture. By forcing the child to focus on these subtle gestures, he begins to learn how better to read the nonverbal gestures of others.

Key Points

- The term Recognize in Sōsh refers to the ability to perceive, to acknowledge, and to accurately identify feelings that both the child and others experience.

- Daily Check-Ins can be a useful exercise to connect behaviors to feelings. Challenges consist of short-term, attainable goals that help keep the child motivated and serve to improve self-esteem.

- Kids who struggle with recognizing their own emotions and nuances of social interactions, and those of others, can benefit from the use of video feedback (Boles & Bowers, 2003). Video cameras are a great way to give kids feedback on their interaction style. Parents are encouraged to be creative and use video taping or audio recording in their everyday interactions with the child.

- Cognitive Behavioral Therapy (CBT) is based on the notion that our thoughts cause our feelings and behaviors, as opposed to external things like people, situations, and events. The way to "dissect" the origin of feelings is to first identify the situation in which these feelings began.

- Mindfulness is bringing one's complete attention to the present experience on a moment-to-moment basis, and paying attention with purpose, in the present moment. Each thought, feeling or sensation is acknowledged, and accepted as it is, for what it is (Bishop et al., 2004).

- The "force a smile" exercise is useful because psychological research (Davis & Palladino, 2000) has demonstrated that the movement of the mouth muscles upward into the smile position releases endorphins into the body that help us feel better.

Chapter Eight

Sōsh in Schools

Sōsh in Schools

When I discuss schools with the families I work with, I provide a disclaimer that I have a love/hate relationship with schools. On the one hand, I have the utmost respect for the teaching profession. My mother was a teacher. I had many wonderful teachers over the course of my 25-year education, from kindergarten through graduate school. However, based on my professional experiences across multiple school districts and states, I have concluded that many schools still do not "get it" when it comes to the vital nature of their role in helping children with social skills difficulties. Further, economic realities, misguided policies, inexperienced administrators, and inconsistent focus often leave otherwise willing educators to fend for themselves when dealing with this difficult, complex and demanding issue. As a result, social skills difficulties are not addressed, they become more pronounced, and the negative cycle continues.

Social difficulties will significantly interfere with a child's academic functioning, no matter how intelligent the child. However, schools often wait until challenges peak to intervene, and some schools don't intervene at all. Social skills are an essential component of a child's education, and difficulties are best addressed as soon as possible (i.e., the younger the better). Schools are either unaware of or don't acknowledge the research on this topic which indicates that children with social skills difficulties are more likely to be rejected by peers and teachers (Vitaro, Brendgren, Larose, & Tremblay, 2005), and are at a higher risk among their peer group for substance use and criminal activity (Eddy, Reid, & Curry, 2002). In addition, if social difficulties are left untreated, mood and/or anxiety symptoms arise, further compounding the situation.

The school setting is the most ideal location for implementing social skills interventions because the school environment contains a built-in peer network as well as numerous opportunities throughout the child's day in which to be social. Schools also employ the necessary professionals to help in the child's social development (i.e., teachers, social workers, school psychologists, special education teachers, teacher consultants, and paraprofessionals). As fertile a ground as the school may provide for improving social skills, however, actually implementing an intervention program is often challenging because of a lack of time, money, and resources.

The frustrating aspect for anyone involved with a child who needs social skills assistance is that the research to date (see Bellini et al., 2007) indicates that current school-based social skills interventions are often only minimally effective. I liken the difficulty in improving social skills schools often experience to a trip to Disneyland without a ticket. There are all sorts of opportunities, but the end result is frustration.

Before becoming too pessimistic, however, let's consider the limitations of the approaches to date. Many of the so-called "ineffective" interventions took place in situations (e.g., a social worker's office or a resource room 1:1 with a teacher consultant or speech therapist) that were away from the child's classroom and natural daily interactions. On the other hand, interventions that were implemented in the child's classroom or throughout the child's day in other areas of the school (e.g., recess or lunch room while the child naturally interacted with the peer group) produced higher intervention effects (Krasny, Williams, Provencal, & Ozonoff, 2003).

When I discuss my concerns and provide recommendations to teachers and school administrators, they typically cite both time and budget challenges, as well as curriculum benchmarks that must be achieved. These are very real obstacles. Despite these limitations, it is still important, indeed vital, for schools to provide a child with social supports. The challenge is to create interventions that are cost effective (i.e., the school doesn't incur any expense) and that maximize the time and opportunities that naturally occur during the school day. Enter the Sōsh Approach.

The Sōsh methodology encourages the use of resources that are readily available in the child's environment (other kids or school staff). Additional resources are not required. Further, by fostering a collaborative environment in school, *all* kids can be coached on their style of interaction. The Sōsh mobile app was developed to make it easier for schools, families, children, and young adults to execute social strategies that otherwise require considerable time, expertise, and resources to accomplish. The primary innovation of the Sōsh mobile application is that it fills commonly occurring social gaps in a "real time" manner to compensate for a lack of formal or manualized social skills education or curriculum.

Because the "neurotypical" brain of the majority of students understands most social rules, norms, and constructs innately, schools have been able to get by without focusing much of their efforts on the explicit teaching and coaching of social skills. Instead, schools have remained focused primarily on academics. Now, however, with diagnostic improvements, earlier detection of delays, and a significant increase of diagnoses that include social skills difficulties, schools can no longer assume that social skills difficulties are not affecting the students in their classrooms.

To the extent that resistance to providing social skills support is about the lack of money, consider how simple, no-cost environmental changes can have a strong influence on children's performance. For example, a year-long experiment is currently being conducted in Michigan where a school district is separating the boys and girls into different classrooms during middle school so they can compare test scores with middle schools where male and female students attend classes together (Steele, 2011). Preliminary teacher testimonials indicate that the female students participate more when in a classroom without boys. They ask more questions, and are more willing to answer questions. A reasonable preliminary hypothesis would be that girls who are separated from boys will have higher test scores than girls who attend class with boys.

This experiment illustrates how a simple environmental change within a school (e.g., separating classes by gender), that does not involve incremental cost, can have a strong effect on outcomes. The social environment should be no exception. There is not a lot of time built into a school day for much beyond academics, and what is especially unfortunate is that there is often an inverse correlation between intelligence and social skills. This means that students can be very bright but still experience significant social difficulties.

I often express my disagreement with schools after they tell families I am working with that their child is "too smart" to qualify for special education services. One of the difficulties of encouraging the school to help the child succeed socially is that technically the school is completing its obligation to provide a Free Appropriate Public Education (FAPE) if the child is learning and is doing reasonably well academically. What I have learned over my years working with kids, and what I try to emphasize to schools, is that it is only a matter of time until academics suffer as a result of the child's inability or difficulty connecting with other kids and teachers. Further, if the child begins to fear school because of feelings of social isolation, or he is being bullied or harassed, teaching this child anything (and sustaining his previously strong academic performance) will be much more difficult. Finally, shouldn't schools be invested in teaching the child to be successful, not only in terms of academics, but also in life? While having high test scores is laudable, being able to connect with others, communicate, problem-solve, function successfully as a member of a team, and engage with others socially are invaluable skill sets as the student seeks independent living and entrance into the job market. Indeed, in the absence of such social skills, academic achievement becomes almost irrelevant.

My general response to the school's argument that "smart" does not qualify for services is to ask, "What do you do with a person who is confined to a wheelchair but has an Above Average or Superior IQ and achieves straight "A's"? Does that level of intellect and academic performance mean that you are not going to allow accommodations for the child's mobility issues?" Whether you can't get to school because of a physical disability, or are avoiding school due to psychological stress and anxiety secondary to social skills delays, the end result is the same: you are not in school, you are not learning, performance suffers, and the risk for dropout increases.

Although special education law is outside of the scope of this book, you may wish to mention to the school official who tries to reject social skills support or other services for your child because he is not failing, that current law is not supportive. According to Individuals with Disabilities Education Act (IDEA) regulation 300.101(c), a school must provide special education to a child with a disability even though the child has not failed or been retained in a course or grade, and is advancing from grade to grade (Wright & Wright, 2007). The word "disability" in this statute indicates that the child must have a classification from the school in order to even begin the discussion of services.

Whenever it is possible (based upon a valid psychological diagnosis or educational classification) to begin an Individualized Education Program (IEP) or Section 504 Plan to help implement social supports for the child, the better are the chances of success. The Individualized Education Program (IEP) and Section 504 Plan are similar in that both require a diagnostic classification by the school. It is important to remember that schools only classify (e.g., "Autism," "Other Health Impairment," and "Specific Learning Disability"-there are currently 13 possible classifications) and do not provide medical or psychological diagnoses. Instead, their classification determines eligibility, and informs and ultimately determines the types of services for which the child is eligible. However, the school must consider any outside diagnoses and reports when determining eligibility for services and accommodations once eligibility has been established.

The IEP is a contractual document that requires annual meetings as well as assessments that, depending on the school district, are updated at specified intervals. IEP accommodations often include therapy services that are paid for by the school district (e.g., speech therapy, occupational therapy, social work). A parent is permitted to request meetings (always do this in writing) to amend the IEP throughout the school year. The Section 504 Plan provides a list of recommendations that do not require incremental costs but can be useful to the student throughout the course of the school day (e.g., preferential seating, additional time to complete a test).

Keep in mind that if you are the parent of a child who is having social difficulties but is doing well academically, it may be difficult during the earlier grades to get formal accommodations. It is typically not until the middle school years that schools begin to realize the extent to which these social difficulties interfere with academic performance.

Regarding school intervention, families should request that:

- Services are specifically described on the student's Individualized Education Program (IEP).

- Anyone responsible for implementing the social skills services must have knowledge about both social skills development and the specifics of implementing the services. You can offer school staff a copy of this book if you think it may be helpful in this regard.

- Services are provided at the necessary rate and intensity to be effective. One or two visits with a social worker each month will probably not meet necessary criteria. Daily contact may be required to meet necessary rate and intensity criteria. If staff are not available at the required rate, then the use of peer supports are indicated, with periodic staff check-ins and training of the peer group.

- Interventions are delivered in authentic locations such as playgrounds, classrooms, lunch rooms, etc. rather than in the social worker's office or a resource room.

Hopefully, schools will recognize the potential significant value of resources such as the Sōsh mobile application and allow students to incorporate this into their everyday academics. This may even be accomplished outside the scope of what might otherwise be required for a formal IEP. Thus, those bright students who do not qualify for special education services might be permitted to incorporate an accommodation that is funded by the family. Parents can choose to purchase the iPad 2 or iPod Touch as well as the Sōsh application. The school would simply need to determine rules and boundaries around the use of the device during the school day.

School staff can be assured that the Sōsh application's sole purpose is to help students navigate social interactions throughout the day and gather information which will ultimately benefit the child, the family, and the school. It really is a win-win situation. The school can save time and resources by allowing the child to use this technology during the school day, perhaps providing brief check-ins on the progress. At the same time, the family receives updates on how their child is progressing socially at school (via email, feedback and archive features built into the application), and can troubleshoot and tweak their approach accordingly. Also, the app can be used during the most ideal times throughout the school day (e.g., lunch, recess, transitions, quiet time) to avoid interfering with progress toward academic goals.

If, in the long run, it is determined that a formalized special education plan (i.e., IEP or Section 504) needs to be implemented, then the Sōsh application can also serve as a way to gather data to begin this process and inform the process during annual meetings and reevaluations. Students are able to archive and email their data to any interested parties as necessary (i.e., teachers, parents). If you have the need (and approval for) an IEP or Section 504, the Sōsh app contains a variety of school-based strategies to help the child, especially in the areas of organization, processing, and planning ahead for academic work as well as social skills. Parents are encouraged to share the contents of this book, and especially this chapter, with schools so that they are aware that you are being advised on the appropriate steps to take to improve the child's social skills over the course of the school day. In the event that you and your child's school are interested in developing a plan for the school day, the following sections can help you begin this process.

Individualized Education Program (IEP) and Section 504 Plan

As previously defined, the Individualized Education Program (IEP) and Section 504 Plan are formalized plans agreed upon with the school to provide the child with some level of assistance or intervention over the course of the school day.

If you are informed by a private professional that your child is eligible for special education services because of a diagnosis that fits into one of the current special education classifications, or if you believe this to be true and the school refuses services, there are a number of options available to you. Although an in-depth discussion of how to navigate this process is outside the scope of this book, you are encouraged to *put all communication with the school in writing.* You are also encouraged to find a special education advocate to work with you, either by asking other parents who have utilized such a service or doing a district or internet search for advocates in your area. School districts keep the names of advocates on file if you feel comfortable asking them for assistance. You may also need to seek out an attorney to represent you or request mediation services, depending on the school's response to your requests. If you are interested in specific information on special education law, an excellent internet resource is www.wrightslaw.com. There are also free apps on the iTunes Store pertaining to IEPs (e.g., *IEP Checklist*) that can be utilized in meetings, as well as books and guides that can be found in the special education section at your local bookstore.

In the meantime, while you are working to get the school on board to provide services, I encourage you to push for social accommodations that do not involve incremental cost and that do not require any formal special education plan or paperwork. These approaches include peer supports that utilize the built-in community of peers. Keep in mind that you will have no legal outlet to assure that the provision of peer supports is consistent and sustained in the absence of a formal special education plan, such as an IEP. Thus, you are going to need to have a positive relationship with school personnel and know how to keep the plan active via check-in and follow-up once it begins. The Sōsh app is one of the easiest ways to accomplish this, given that it guides the student without needing to draw on the resources of the school. The school need only provide supervision and some support regarding the peer group involvement. This book can also serve as a guide to aid school personnel in the process, if necessary.

Positive Peer Supports

The earlier that you request the assistance of the peer group to help a fellow student with social skills difficulty, the greater the level of empathy, assistance, and support you can expect from that peer group. The goal is to create a culture, or a community of peer support, that is not geared only toward kids with social difficulties. Imagine the ripple effect of that type of approach! Besides, this generalized approach also works very well, especially with regard to reducing bullying, encouraging problem solving and teamwork, and encouraging inclusion for cooperative activities. It sounds like common sense that a problem-solving, teamwork-oriented approach increases and improves student relationships and school performance, yet some schools fail to approach their curricula in this manner. Instead, some schools continue to opt for an "every man for himself" style of making it through the day. This is likely the same phenomena that plays itself out in very large families, where there are simply too many kids to permit the necessary individual parental attention. What often happens in large families, however, is that siblings support one another, and more advanced siblings teach those who have yet to learn the same skills.

Cooperative Learning

Cooperative learning strategies recognize that differences exist among students and that many students do not fit neatly within the traditional, independence-driven model. Working in small groups and using cooperative strategies encourages all students to:

- Think aloud, take risks, and develop deeper understandings and higher order thinking.
- Become more self-confident.
- Develop language skills (because student input into activities is encouraged as part of the exercises).
- Improve their relationships with other students and with their teachers.

For schools interested in incorporating some cooperative learning strategies or social skills lessons into their curriculum, the following exercises may be a good place to start.

Placemat and Round Robin

This activity is designed to allow for each individual's thinking, perspective and voice to be heard, recognized, and explored. The more that peers hear from each other, the more opportunities they have to get to know one another.

- Divide the class into groups of four.
- Allocate one piece of butcher's paper to each group.
- Ask each group to draw the following diagram on the paper.
- Select a topic.

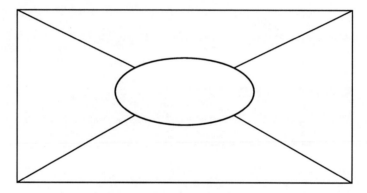

1. The outer spaces are for each participant to write his thoughts about the topic.
2. Conduct a "Round Robin" (students give their opinions verbally around the circle or group and all members contribute) so that each participant can share his views.
3. The circle in the middle is to write down (by the nominated scribe) the common points made by the participants.
4. Each group then reports the common points to the whole group or class.

Plus, Minus, Intriguing (PMI)

A PMI (**P**lus, **M**inus, **I**ntriguing) is used for affective processing to discuss the positives (pluses), negatives (minuses) and questions (intriguing points) about a lesson, concept, or issue. While highly effective in a group, this exercise is also useful when working 1:1 with a child about a specific experience from their day (e.g., going to school).

What I liked *Pluses (+)*	
What I didn't like *Minuses (-)*	
What I thought was intriguing *Questions or thoughts*	

T Chart for Problem and Solution Identification

T Charts (named for the shape of the chart) are used to examine a particular problem or issue. The dilemma or problem is identified and written in the left column (younger kids can draw pictures instead of using words), and possible solutions are discussed and written in the right column. The child is asked to select the solution most likely to solve the problem.

Problem	Solution

T Chart for Effective Listening

To explore effective listening skills, ask students to complete a T Chart in table form. The charts may be displayed in the classroom and used as a reference point during classroom activities.

Effective Listening	
Looks like:	**Sounds like:**
▪ Head nodding. ▪ Eye contact. ▪ Concentrating. ▪ Using my face to show that I am interested in what the speaker is saying.	▪ Only one voice speaking. ▪ Words like "Yes" and "I see" to support the speaker. ▪ Quiet voices. ▪ Polite language.

Y Charts

Y Charts are an extension of T Charts. These can be used to identify aspects of specific behaviors by specifying what the behavior looks like, feels like, and sounds like. Consider the behavior of listening as outlined above. The person **feels** good learning something new, **looks like** he is listening because he is nodding his head and looking at the person talking, and **sounds** quiet.

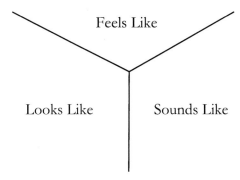

Feels Like

Looks Like   Sounds Like

Venn Diagram (Comparison Charts)

Venn diagrams assist students in identifying similarities and differences between ideas, concepts or problems. The similarities are recorded in the intersection of the two circles. The differences are recorded in the outer sections of the two circles.

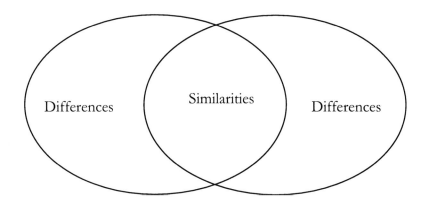

The Importance of Cooperation

A famous psychological study illustrates the importance of peers working together. Sherif, Harvey, White, Hood, and Sherif (1961) studied intergroup conflict in a classic study called the "Robbers Cave" experiment (named for the state park in Oklahoma where the study took place) which demonstrated that when a group of kids is faced with a problem in which they must work together (or else the problem cannot be solved), it fosters a sense of cooperation. The children in this study were led to believe they were campers at a summer camp. They were divided into two "rival" groups and were encouraged by the researchers (ostensibly, the camp "counselors") to compete against each other in various events. When the rival groups were forced into a problem-solving situation after days of competition (pulling a "broken down" camp truck back to camp, which required all of the kids to work together), the result was that the kids set aside their prior differences and group rivalries to complete a common goal.

At the very least, the idea of kids getting to know each other on a variety of different levels helps contribute to a more supportive and collaborative classroom environment. Just as intergroup conflict can be created by adults (as seen by what the researchers posing as camp counselors did in the Robbers Cave experiment), cooperative interactions free from conflict can also be facilitated by adults (as demonstrated in the same study). Bullies typically target kids who are isolated or whom they know little about aside from some "weak" or "vulnerable" quality. Having kids work together on various projects during the day can lead to a decrease in bullying. Kids should be encouraged to interact with each other throughout the day on projects, facilitated by the teacher, using methods such as those described above.

Tell Peers? Tell Your Child?

This question of whether to tell the peer group about any specific diagnosis that contributes to social difficulties is common among parents and teachers alike. Of course, this decision always depends on the wishes of the child and the family. Teachers will not notify peers of the child's difficulty without the family's expressed consent. I find that parents and teachers can successfully navigate this discussion early in the child's life (e.g., kindergarten through second grade) with the child's peers using simple, concrete language to describe the social difficulty. For example, just as some kids in the class have freckles, or glasses, or brown hair, or green eyes, this otherwise smart, funny, caring student needs help learning how to play with others. It may be helpful to ask other parents or teachers who have had these discussions with a group of kids what they found to be useful.

The feedback that I often receive from families is that the younger the peer group is informed, the better the outcomes. This may be because the level of empathy and willingness to lend support is higher among younger children. Also, if the group will remain classmates through elementary school, it can be useful to get its support early before behaviors cause distraction.

The peer group is typically aware of difficulties (i.e., referring to the child as "strange" or "weird"). Some parents tell me that peers will approach them at the end of a school day and innocently ask why the child does certain things in class. This type of feedback or descriptors of the child's behavior (e.g., "weird") are often what children say, not to be mean, but as a means of trying to describe what they are observing. Sometimes if you give a name to the difficulty, it's easier for the peer group to understand. In the absence of a label, or if you are not comfortable with this approach, then you are encouraged to describe the specific behaviors that are creating difficulty (e.g., "He wants to play with you guys but you might notice that he stays away and watches what you are doing. So, if you could ask him to play every now and then, it would really help and he would really like it").

With regard to children experiencing social difficulties, many are aware that there is something "different" about them (i.e., they need to work harder than their peers to "keep up" during social interactions), and may even ask questions about their situation or become sad/mad about their situation. Determining whether or not to discuss a specific diagnosis with them involves many factors, including the child's age and cognitive level of development. When in doubt, or if there are concerns about using diagnostic terminology with a child, always describe the child's talents and strengths in combination with areas in which they will need to work harder. By describing specific behaviors (e.g., "Sometimes you become so interested in what you are discussing that others don't have a turn to talk"), you begin to identify areas to practice skills rather than using a broad diagnostic term that may confuse or offend the child.

Lunch Groups

Positive peer supports can become members of lunch groups often referred to as a "Lunch Bunch." This is basically a group of kids who agree to eat together daily. This can occur in the cafeteria, or, depending on the school layout, can be in a quieter environment (e.g., classroom or library), especially if there are sensory issues to consider (e.g., noise sensitivity or aversion to crowds). In general, a lunch group is a supportive group of people that connects with one another over lunch and can get to know one another well by meeting during each lunch period over a period of months, a semester, or even a year. Some schools rotate participation in the peer group so that all kids are involved and a particular child is not identified. Having an adult facilitate and supervise these lunch groups provides the necessary feedback and facilitation, although some group time without adults (depending on the age and level of the group) is also useful. In the absence of a Lunch Bunch, having supervision in the lunch room is often useful, especially teachers or staff who are willing to go around to tables and talk (or even briefly sit) with the kids in their natural seating arrangements, making students feel more comfortable and possibly facilitating relationships in the process.

Recess

The playground can be an ideal place to practice social skills, provided there is adequate supervision and coaching. In the absence of coaching or mediation by adults or positive peer models, the child is not going to "figure it out" simply by exposure. As stated earlier, although I may want my child to be able to swim, I can't just throw him into the pool and hope that he will figure it out. The same logic applies to the playground. Supervision and coaching of social skills is essential. Recess is a wonderful opportunity each day to work on social skills and connections with peers. Unfortunately, recess is also a time in which teachers attend to administrative matters, and schools typically cannot afford to have a playground proctor. If schools utilize a volunteer parent or staff member to be on the playground, their role is often focused on safety and basic supervision of the children (e.g., watching to make sure that strange adults don't enter the playground or making sure that kids remain on the school's property) and they rarely have the time to help with social interactions.

Instead of focusing our efforts on what activities the children could do together (which may be a big step), the focus of the Sōsh approach, initially, is to encourage and teach social skills development among kids. This approach is not just for the child who is having difficulty, but for all kids who can benefit from improved social interactions with one another. In other words, Sōsh can be applied with *all* kids. Students develop new social skills when a teacher (usually an adult, but possibly a peer) leads them through social interactions. A teacher can offer various levels of assistance over the course of numerous social interactions. The goal is to allow the child to do as much as he can on his own, and then to intervene and provide assistance when it is needed so the social interaction can be successfully completed.

Having an available adult or peer (who is capable of coaching) to guide a group of kids through the *See One, Do One, Teach One* approach is essential. Don't be afraid to combine boys and girls together, especially during the younger grades as girls are often excellent peer mentors for boys with social difficulties. Kids can even volunteer to be a group leader during a recess period and choose an activity they will teach the group. Adults can be available to supervise as the children attempt to complete the activity. The group members can then show the adults what they have learned as they *Teach One* to the adult. Consider the cooperative game of "Sardines." This can be played anywhere, indoors or out. The goal is similar to "Hide and Seek," except that "it" hides first. Everyone else then tries to find "it." When someone finds "it," they hide with "it" in the same spot. The game ends when everyone finds the hiding spot of "it."

Back-and-Forth Communication Log

Back-and-forth communication between school and home is essential and extends across all stages of school development. Effective two-way partnerships between home and school are built through input regarding the child's learning, sharing and listening to concerns, inviting feedback about classroom and home activities and, where appropriate, eliciting active support. This communication establishes a relationship of trust and support. Open and consistent communication helps to keep everyone "in the loop" and helps avoid any misunderstandings, while also providing home and school with reciprocal "heads up" information.

One way to help facilitate this communication process is to keep a log. This can be as simple as a notebook that has columns for notes related to home and school. Parents can fill out the log in the morning before dropping the child off at the bus or driving the child to school. The parent may document things that went well, things that were difficult for the child at home, and other behavioral notes. At school, the teacher can help the child complete it (or complete it without the child) before dismissal each day. School feedback can include items such as what went well, what was difficult, points earned, homework for the evening, missing assignments, and social skills practiced today, to name a few. Some families have created their own systems with check boxes and pictures to represent specific behaviors that were displayed on any given day. Only the parents and the school will know which system, from simple to elaborate, will work best.

Children find it useful to acknowledge something that has not gone well in the back-and-forth log, but also to verbalize what did go well. I recommend a 2:1 ratio of good things that happened during the day to things that did not go well (e.g., *Two Roses and One Thorn Game*). The child is instructed to list the "bad thing" or "thorn" first because children, especially those with social difficulties, can often easily identify something negative from the day. In fact, they often have four or five things they would like to list but they should be required to pick the thing that really bothered them most about the day. The two other notes are positive things, the "roses," that went well. It can be something as small or simple such as, "Billy said 'Hi' to me," or, "I got to take a turn during recess." It does not need to be a huge accomplishment, but the process is designed to remind a child to recognize and acknowledge that although things do not always go as planned or as well as he would have liked, the day was not *all* bad and some things can (and did) go well.

The back-and-forth log should not be a burden to the school when it is used properly. It should not take more than a few minutes to complete at the end of each day. Seek out the appropriate staff member to complete it each day and it will eventually become a comfortable and familiar part of the daily routine. Some schools have tried to use face cartoons with a happy smile, frown, and straight line for a mouth (i.e., "okay" day) as their back-and-forth log. Emotional representations in graphic form may work for younger kids, but without any qualifiers or additional information, they are not particularly useful for parents. Thus, if the school uses a check mark, stars, red/yellow/green, or faces as a way of documenting the day, written comments of substance beyond "Good Day" should be included.

The Sōsh mobile application has this back-and-forth capability built into it. The *Feedback* page quickly and easily allows teachers or other individuals in the child's life to provide feedback. Also, if the child wants to provide personal feedback, he can do that on the *Feedback* page or he can document some of the events from their day in the *Journal* section of the Sōsh app. There is also an audio record feature if the child has difficulties with typing or spelling. This *Feedback* can then be instantly emailed so that parents can have it before the child arrives home.

Separation between School and Home Behavior

During the early elementary school years, it is imperative to separate school and home behavior. Do not try to discipline for things that happened at school once the child returns home for the day. When it comes to consequences, it is important to remember: **The longer that you wait between a behavior occurring and the administration of the consequence, the less effective the consequence.** So if the child misbehaves at 10 a.m., arrives home at 4 p.m., and is disciplined at home, the connection between the early misbehavior and the late consequence is lost. As a result, the consequence will lack power and effectiveness and may fuel frustration and hostility.

The reverse logic would be downright silly. Imagine your child had a rough night and was misbehaving before going to bed. You drop your child off at school the next morning and say to the teacher, "Now would you make sure that you discipline Billy today and give him some extra work because he was really difficult last night." The teacher would look at you like you're crazy! Whenever possible, the school should manage behaviors *while the child is still at school.* Dangerous and threatening behaviors that call for suspensions and expulsions are obvious exceptions to this rule. However, nothing is more irritating than when a parent receives a phone call or email saying that the school doesn't know what to do about a child's behavior. That is both nonproductive and indicative of a lack of understanding of behavioral strategies, especially if there are supports (e.g., IEP) in place for that particular child.

It is generally not appropriate for schools to request that parents come to pick up their children from school because they are misbehaving, unless the behavior is dangerous. What happens during the school day should be addressed using the school's expertise. Then, at the end of the day, concerns can be discussed in-depth with the family once all the data from that day has been collected.

Middle/Junior High School

Your anxiety is likely to increase with the very mention of middle school. You may even have flashbacks of your own middle school days as you consider your child's middle school experience. This is the period of development that we would like to just fast forward through or avoid altogether, but unfortunately we all go through it. I don't believe it is a rite of passage to be completely humiliated, teased, and bullied during middle school, but this style of interaction is unfortunately at its peak during these years and parents and teachers have to be fully aware when it's happening and how to respond. To make matters even more complicated for the child experiencing social difficulties, even good friends do tease each other, or otherwise give each other a hard time. Boys that I see in my practice, who are not experiencing social skills difficulties, report that this type of teasing is an indication of a close friendship when peers can comfortably "poke fun" at one another. For the child with limited social awareness or trouble reading cues, these affectionate "jabs" may be misperceived as insults or bullying. This is why parents must be cautious when the child returns home and begins to speak of others "teasing" him. Be sure to get all of the facts together and investigate with the school before allowing your emotions to escalate in response to the child's claims of harassment. If the situation does need to addressed, then do so, but recognize that it may be simply the child's misperception, and the peers may have merely been trying to engage with the child in a sarcastic or playful fashion.

Hopefully, the child will enter middle school with a peer group that knows him well, and a peer group known to the parents, as this can alleviate frequent misunderstandings and can also provide opportunities for peer allies to provide feedback to the family (i.e., "a set of eyes on the inside"). If your child is entering into a new building for middle school with unfamiliar students, then do your best to get involved with parent organizations or other school activities (e.g., fundraisers, carnivals, book fairs) in order to meet other parents and other kids. The more involved you are, the more aware you will be of opportunities to suggest and even facilitate social connections for your child.

During middle school, many kids face prepubescent immaturity, hostility, and animosity in which "power grabs" occur. Students try to obtain status with one another and in their groups. These adolescents are now looking for common ground between peers in ways that differ from their previous methods. Common ground is now about value systems, such as where your family comes from, or how well you keep up with the trends, and what you say (or how you say it). "Beware if you don't fit in" should be a sign on the schoolyard fence. Even within groups of close-knit peers, there exists considerable animosity and insecurity. Kids learn quickly that you don't want to stray too far from the ordinary or acceptable and you certainly don't want to do or say anything that might make you stand out in an unacceptable way.

Animosity is especially prominent in young girls who are becoming more covert in their operations. Boys who get into conflict during this time may resolve it with a shoving match or other physical or verbal altercation. Girls, on the other hand, will opt for more indirect, relationally aggressive means to "take care of business." This may be in the form of starting rumors or spreading gossip, trying to embarrass or humiliate a person in front of the peer group, and a variety of other relationally aggressive strategies. If you are raising a 'tween or even a teen girl, I recommend you read *Odd Girl Out*, *Tripping the Prom Queen*, and/or *Surviving Ophelia* with your daughter and discuss the book to open a dialogue about this style of aggression. This may help prepare your daughter for what is unfortunately nearly inevitable among girls.

There is an increased potential for bullying during the middle school years that necessitates school bullying initiatives for the entire student population. The message must be clear: Bullying is NOT a rite of passage, it is NEVER acceptable, and WON'T be tolerated. Schools are beginning to implement Bully-Victim-Bystander programs that encourage witnesses or bystanders to speak up and protect the victim. Bullies immediately lose their power when others refuse to join in the harassment and defend the victim.

Because bullying is a covert activity, adults seldom see it occurring. This may be one reason why schools would deny it happens at all. There are other reasons why bullying can go unchallenged in schools:

- School staff may misinterpret aggressive bullying as harmless physical horseplay and therefore fail to intervene.
- When questioned by adults, victims may deny that bullying is taking place. Victims may lie about the bullying because: 1) they fear retaliation from the bully for telling, 2) the bully is present during the questioning, or 3) they do not believe that the adults in the school will be able to stop the bullying.
- There may be too few supervising adults in those unstructured settings where bullying is most likely to occur (e.g., gym, lunch room, playground), or those supervising adults may not be properly trained to intervene early and assertively when they observe questionable behavior.

In general, schools are becoming more attuned to bully prevention and its importance with some schools instituting zero tolerance programs that result in suspensions or even expulsions for bullying. I encourage families to teach their children effective bully responses in the home as well, and never depend only on the school to teach these strategies. If your child is being bullied, gather as much information as you can and schedule a meeting with the school to discuss it in a calm manner. Or, if you know the family of the child who is being accused of doing the bullying, you can decide whether you would be comfortable discussing the matter outside of school. The following are some strategies to review with your child:

- Help your child practice what to say to the bully so he will be prepared the next time.
- Help your child practice being assertive. The simple act of insisting that the bully leave him alone may have a surprising effect. Explain to your child that the bully's true goal is to get a response.
- Encourage your child to be with friends or trusted peers when traveling back and forth from school, during shopping trips, or on other outings. Bullies are less likely to pick on a child in a group.

Drugs/Alcohol

A major concern beginning during the middle school years is the use of drugs and alcohol. I will touch on this rather large issue only as it relates to children with social and emotional difficulties. A more in-depth discussion of this topic is outside the scope of this book and should be pursued aggressively if you have any concerns.

Drug and alcohol use is more likely to occur if a child is having self-esteem concerns and not receiving appropriate treatment to address areas of difficulty that are adversely affecting his life. This is especially true for a child who lacks coping strategies to deal with negative emotions. When exposed to drugs or alcohol, for example, feelings of anxiety are typically reduced. The individual may then continue to use substances for the same desired effect. This is typically referred to as "self-medicating." This is why a good treatment specialist is important to determine the need for medications or counseling. Preemptively talking with kids about the dangers of drugs and alcohol as well as alternative, positive coping strategies will help keep the dialogue open and ongoing. Further, monitoring peer pressure experienced by a child having social difficulties is essential given the higher risk for peer pressure for such children.

Organization

In the beginning of fifth and sixth grade, and even to some extent beginning at the end of third grade through fourth grade, the organizational demands increase in school. This need for better organization is essential not only to academic success, but also for kids to navigate different teachers, different classes in different rooms, and different organizational structures. Teachers vary in their approaches to homework completion (e.g., show your work) and the materials that are required. The system used to document assignments for each class usually begins with a daily planner. Some schools make using a planner mandatory while others leave it up to the child to decide the best way for them to organize. Technology has tremendous potential to help keep a person organized. Websites and mobile apps such as *Dropbox* and *Evernote* allow individuals to organize every facet of their lives (if they choose), and share this information with others as required.

It is essential to prepare the child as much as possible and provide resources to address any organizational difficulties. Study skills classes are often available in middle schools and high schools. Children with organizational difficulties should be encouraged to approach planning and organization as if it were an academic subject. It is important that key concepts and methods from study skills classes be communicated with parents so the concepts can be practiced across all environments for consistency. Although study skills classes can provide important information to students about academically relevant organizational strategies, the student may need ongoing assistance with the application of these strategies. Thus, individual application of strategies, with review, cuing, and generalization should be strongly considered.

Difficulties with organization and planning may be an indication of an underlying executive function difficulty, which is often present among kids with social skills delays. One of my favorite practical references on addressing daily executive function difficulties in kids is a book called *Smart but Scattered* (Dawson & Guare, 2009), that you may want to review. The book does a good job of separating executive function into components and providing useful and valuable strategies. Another option is to explore the educational resources in your area. It may be helpful to employ academic tutors to generate organizational strategies for the child. College students majoring in Education can be a useful and potentially inexpensive resource for tutoring. Plus, a middle school student might view it as "cool" to work with someone in college. Retired teachers or the child's favorite teacher from a previous grade may also be good options for tutoring organization or study skills.

If you are interested in measuring how your child "thinks" in terms of academics, memory, attention, processing speed, and organization, a neuropsychological evaluation may be helpful. This evaluation can profile an individual's strengths and weaknesses and identify how they perform relative to their age and grade. This can be a valuable assessment battery, providing a wealth of information for parents and students, especially as a child is approaching high school or college and there is a need to understand areas of growth. A licensed psychologist with expertise in this area is the person to consult as they are the only professionals who receive this training and who are authorized and licensed to administer such tests.

Homework

It is important to think about what your student is doing, how he is doing it, and the way(s) in which he learns best. If he memorizes best by singing a song, utilize that technique. If rhymes or mnemonics work well, use them to enhance recall. If organization is easiest with folders, use them. It doesn't matter what the approach looks like, as long as it's effective. Once a system that works is in place, stick with it.

For families dealing with a child who is having difficulties with planning, organization, and assignment/homework completion I suggest considering the following:

Elementary-Middle School Homework

- **Establish a Homework Schedule**. Setting aside a time each day when homework will be completed is helpful. For example, a one hour block for homework may be set each night at 7 p.m. If the child typically has 30 minutes of work, this allows ample time for completion. If he finishes the work early, he can read a book or review the completed homework for accuracy until the hour is over. This way, he understands there is no incentive to rush the completion of work.

- **Don't Hover Over a Child During Homework.** This is called "helicopter parenting." Have the child complete his work and then check in or ask questions when he has questions or feels stuck, or after work has been completed, to ensure accuracy.

- **If You *Must* Check the Child's Work**, be sure to comment on the correct items first. Too often, we focus on the errors and don't focus on what the child did well. Keep his confidence up whenever possible, especially during this age.

High School Homework

- **Encourage the Child to Check the Online Homework Portal** (if utilized by the school). The child should do this on his own and then establish a time you will log on (preferably with him) to review progress. This way, he knows when assignments must be turned in and can coordinate with teachers to have the information updated prior to parental review (another important step on the road to independence-advocating for oneself and problem-solving with adults other than parents). I usually recommend parents review online homework portals every other Wednesday. Weekends need to be enjoyable and logging on to potentially see bad news is a bad idea. The middle of the week gives the child enough time in the beginning of the week to catch up, and enough time at the end of the week to make up work.

- **Back Off!** If the child does not have any learning difficulties or associated concerns that would require more support and intervention, it is best to let him handle academic difficulties on his own while you focus on responsibilities and rules of the home such as curfew, cell phone/electronics use, etc. If after a decent period of time (i.e., one quarter), the child continues to struggle in school, then a professional consult may be warranted to rule out learning or emotional contributions to the difficulties in school.

After-School Activity

I always encourage at least one structured and time-limited (i.e., meets one hour each week) after-school activity that allows a child social exposure and varied experience outside of the home. If the activity is school related, there is a built-in peer network of familiar faces and more opportunities to practice social interactions. Further, this helps to establish common ground so that when the child sees a person from his after-school group walking in the hall during school, he now has something in common that he can discuss or use to facilitate new discussion.

Not Just Doing: Observe and Report

Improving social functioning not only involves going out and doing things, but also observing. During elementary school, but especially during middle and high school, there are many opportunities for observing social interactions (e.g., on the bleachers at basketball games, in the lunchroom). The child does not necessarily need to carry around a notebook, but it is helpful to note in some way what is observed.

This is where the Sōsh application can be a useful tool because it provides a socially acceptable medium to complete this exercise. The individual is able to record notes onto his device for archive and later review. Anyone observing the person simply sees him looking at his device and typing. No one knows that he is working on social skills. The Sōsh application also goes one step further by allowing you to document your own interactions with video or voice recordings so that you can review them later with a family member or therapist. When the child is younger, provided the school allows it, the Sōsh app becomes a portal into the social world and all you need is an iPad 2, iPhone, or iPod Touch and a willingness to use the Sōsh application regularly.

No one flinches in the middle school years or beyond when someone is using one of these devices because there are a number of things the student could be doing, all of which are perfectly acceptable. Most children this age are texting, checking e-mail, or looking at their calendars. No one is looking over the student's shoulder with any awareness that he is documenting his social experiences. He can be busily taking social skills notes, and looking like any other student, deeply involved in typing on an electronic device.

Key Points

- An Individualized Education Program (IEP) or Section 504 Plan may be necessary to ensure that a child receives the necessary accommodations and supports throughout the school day. This is more difficult to accomplish if social skills are the primary area of concern.

- Cooperative Learning is essential for social skills development among children of all ages, regardless of their level of social development.

- Peer Supports can be a powerful tool to help the child with social skills difficulties, and do not require funding from the school. These peers can be especially valuable to the child during recess and lunch, times that tend to be unsupervised and unstructured and where difficulties can occur.

- Bully-victim-bystander programs are a necessary component of all educational programs for children.

- Children need additional support with organization and homework completion as they enter the third and fourth grades, and especially in middle school. Parents and teachers must find a balance between helping and hovering, and also keep in close contact to "bridge the gap" between school and home.

- Older children need to observe and monitor the social interactions of others and document their findings to help facilitate the learning process (i.e., what they are expected to be doing relative to their peers' level of social functioning).

Chapter Nine

Barriers to Social Success

Barriers to Social Success

Children and families who experience social skills difficulties face numerous obstacles. The work required to teach social skills is demanding and often frustrating. Typically, children make large, noticeable gains followed by periods in which progress seems to have stalled. Change requires motivation and effort. Depending on the demeanor and personality of the child and how long he has experienced social difficulties, the task of accomplishing social skills goals can be painstaking.

Throughout this book you have been introduced to a variety of strategies designed to improve social skills. The Sōsh approach stresses that, in addition to implementing these interventions, it is important to be prepared for factors that may interrupt or interfere with success. This chapter reviews the most common barriers to social success. If you begin to experience frustration or think, "This isn't working," I urge you to return to this chapter to determine if one of these barriers is getting in the way. As is always the case when trying to guide a child through this difficult social journey, having a qualified professional on your team with expertise in this area is essential.

Setting the Bar Too High

When setting goals, it is vital for children and parents to keep expectations realistic. Start small. There is no drive-thru, magical, one-size-fits-all, "happy pill" approach to address social difficulties. Progress is a direct result of the work put in. If you want to lose weight, you go to the gym and work out repeatedly, you eat well, and you see results. Meeting your goals will require time, patience, and effort.

Too often, children become overwhelmed and expend their energy early in the process. When running a marathon, a runner does not begin at a sprinter's pace. Children with social skills difficulties often spend considerable energy trying to remember all of the rules regarding how to be social, including maintaining eye contact, turn-taking, and greeting others. This is a lot to keep track of initially, and leaves a child with little energy for execution of these strategies. Children need to be able to pick one technique to work on, and begin to demonstrate competence in that area before adding more skills to the list.

The example that I often use when working with adolescent males who are beginning to express an interest in females who may be "out of their league" is borrowed from the movie, *A Beautiful Mind*. The main character (John Nash) is at a nightclub with several of his male friends when a beautiful blonde girl walks into the bar with several of her female friends. John determines the following in his mind as he lets the audience in on his thinking:

> If we [John and his friends] all go for the blond, we will block each other and not a single one of us is going to get her. So then we will go for her friends, but they will all give us the cold shoulder because no one likes to be second choice. But what if none of us goes for the blonde? We won't get in each other's way and we won't insult the other girls. It's the only way to win.

This example demonstrates the importance of keeping expectations realistic. But beyond that, individuals must consider the probability of having success in social interactions, romantic or otherwise. If the odds are in the child's favor, such as approaching a group of peers who know each other well, then the approach makes sense. When the outcome odds are unfavorable, the child runs the risk of becoming frustrated when things do not go as planned.

Children with social skills difficulties often experience rejection and suffer a loss of self-esteem when they are unsuccessful at engaging others in social interactions. Repeated rejection reduces energy and interferes with motivation toward future social skills practice, and thus opportunities for success.

Consider, for example, the teenager who tries, on a number of occasions, to approach a group of peers in the hallway between classes to say "Hello," but the group ignores the overture or laughs at the teen. It is only a matter of time before this teenager will generalize this experience to all group interactions and avoid initiating them in the future. However, the teen must consider the group that he will try to approach and the timing as well as the method of approach. Walking up to a group of cheerleaders with whom you have never interacted and asking them about Star Wars is not recommended. For the younger child, perhaps preschool age, running up to unfamiliar kids in a store and hugging them is not advised either.

Kids also need to understand that they cannot sit in their basement playing video games or engage in other solitary activities every weekend and expect to make friends. Kids want the process of improving social functioning to begin automatically, proceed without much effort, and progress quickly. In our society, individuals want outcomes quickly and without much work. Unfortunately, in order to obtain most good things in life, effort is essential, and this is especially the case when working to improve social skills. Be prepared to crawl before you walk, and be prepared to ask for help.

For kids who struggle socially, parents need to nurture and explicitly coach these skills as explained in detail earlier in the **Development** chapter of this book. Time after time, I work with children who are not making gains because, although they have been encouraged or pushed to be social, they do not receive sufficient support or guidance. Encouragement is one thing, but enrolling the child into Advanced English Composition before he learns Phonics is going to create problems. Thus, be sure that goals are achievable and reasonable for the child's level of development and abilities.

Another problem, related to how high the bar is set, is the measure of progress. Success must be measured from the start of your social journey, and not in comparison to where/how others may be performing. This is important for both parents and children to recognize. If you are the parent on the playground comparing your child to other children who are naturally social and skilled at social interactions, then you may begin to feel frustrated and potentially even a little sad about your situation. If, however, you notice that your child just said "Hello" back to a child who greeted him, and this was something that your child had never done before, then we have an indicator of some progress relative to the child's baseline of performance.

Another thing to keep in mind is that progress speeds up and slows down at seemingly unpredictable intervals. Thus, if your child makes some considerable gains over a few months and then slows down for a month or so, I am less likely to say, "He is slowing down" and might instead say, "Wow, that was great. You are still working so hard on this stuff!" If progress stalls for extended periods of time (i.e., greater than four months), though, be sure to check in with the child and even an independent professional to be sure that other factors are not interfering with continued success.

Insanity?

Albert Einstein once said, "The definition of insanity is doing the same thing over and over again and expecting different results." Does this apply to the way you or your child approach social skills? I include this potential barrier to social improvement for a couple of reasons. First, at one point or another while trying to help a child with social skills, both the child and adult will feel like they are losing their mind. This is to be expected; you are not going "crazy." I find it useful to warn families of this prior to beginning our work together in my private practice because social skills development is very stressful and exhausting work that can take an emotional and psychological toll. The rewards and payoff for the child (and for any adult involved), however, greatly outweigh the emotional expenses.

Thus, parents must be sure to take care of themselves. Before you take off on an airplane, the flight attendant says, "If you are traveling with a small child and we experience a loss of cabin pressure, place the oxygen mask over yourself first and then attend to your child." This instruction always causes me to think of the importance of taking care of ourselves as adults first so that we can be available to assist our kids. After all, what good are you going to be to your child if you are unconscious due to a loss of cabin pressure (or in the case of social skills work, exhaustion)?

The second reason I include this section is that I often see kids with social difficulties repeating strategies that are not working. Although moving from strategy to strategy too quickly is troublesome, recognizing when something is not working (perhaps the bar has been set too high) and making the necessary changes is essential. Consider, for example, the family who tried very hard to provide their child with social opportunities. However, they continued to choose team sports as the opportunities. Both parents are very athletic and participated in sports during college. Thus, their interest and encouragement in sports involvement is understandable. Unfortunately for the child, he is delayed in his gross motor coordination, and really has no interest in sports. He was more interested in looking for bugs during the soccer game than in the game itself. When they switched to baseball, he became offended that his teammates began cheering, "Hey batter...Hey batter!" because he thought it was rude to try and distract another player. Thus, the bar was set too high and this family was ultimately advised to enroll the child in some individual sports such as swimming, rock climbing, golf, bowling, or fencing (he participated in these one-at-a-time before doing a new one) where he began to thrive. He still had social opportunities with other kids on the team (just not all at the same time), and he was involved in sports, which was important to his parents. He was also able to compare his performance to his own previous scores which kept him motivated to improve and also eliminated any feeling of letting down the team. Indeed, competing against his own average resulted in accountability only to himself, and thus the stress of possibly "letting the team down" due to poor performance was eliminated.

Approach-Avoidance-Ambivalence

Over the course of this book you have read about a "switch" that seems to turn on in a child's brain at around nine years of age. This is when the child begins to want to improve his social skills. The question I often hear after the "switch" turns on is, "Why did my child have some interest in being social for a while, but then give up?" The answer to this question may be best explained by a theory associated with social psychology.

Kurt Lewin (1935) was a social psychologist who established theories about the conflict that humans experience in their daily lives and how they seek to resolve these conflicts. He coined the term "approach-avoidance conflict" which refers to the conflict that people experience when approaching something positive that also has negative elements. For example, the child with social skills difficulty may approach the seemingly desirable situation of making a new friend, but then become anxious thinking of the potentially negative consequences of the peer not wanting to be his friend. The resulting emotional state is one of ambivalence, and questions such as "What should I do?" arise. The shy, adolescent boy who wishes to ask a girl from his math class to the prom fears rejection (the quality he wishes to *avoid*) while also hoping that she will say, "Yes" (the quality he wishes to *approach*). Approach-avoidance conflicts are difficult to resolve. Further, the negative consequences often are only imagined and thus the person may avoid interaction with others because they imagine how "terrible" the result will be.

At times, the parents of this child are also susceptible to the approach-avoidance conflict and may avoid social activities such as play dates or play groups because of the negative results (e.g., the child's behavioral outbursts, stares of other moms). This will ultimately hinder social skills progress, which must be developed among a variety of peers and in a variety of contexts in order for success to be achieved.

For example, let's say you take your young child to a playground, a library group, or a playgroup and he begins to experience a behavioral "meltdown" (e.g., yelling, having a tantrum). The other parents and even some of the other children are now all watching this happen. The child is embarrassing you and giving you plenty of incentive to leave the situation. The question becomes, are you okay leaving with the child for the benefit of your own (or his) comfort? If you go back to your comfortable home environment to avoid stress and conflict, will the child make progress?

The outcome of avoidance in this scenario is that the child is happy (he got his way and was able to leave), Mom and Dad are happy (no more embarrassment), and everybody wins, correct? Not necessarily. In the short-term everyone may feel more comfortable, but over the long-term the child is unlikely to make any social gains and may come to avoid social settings and interactions altogether. It may be useful to think about the process as similar to taking your child to his first pediatrician or dentist appointment. The chances are high that he will scream and yell, or at the very least cry from fear of the unknown, but the child needs to have the exam, the shot, or the teeth cleaning for the sake of his overall health. Thus, the parents must stay the course and the child has to "tough it out." Social exposure may not be nearly as terrible or painful for a child as getting a shot, but the approach should be the same. In other words, it needs to be done despite the protests. Besides, the child recovers and eventually builds up "immunity" by repeated exposures. He begins to learn and know what to expect. Further, his confidence improves and more advanced social skills can be developed by building on this sense of accomplishment that results from facing a difficult situation and persevering. No pain, no gain.

A disclaimer is in order here. First, avoidance is not always the way these approach-avoidance conflicts play out when families are attempting to address social difficulties, especially around others. I work with many families who could not care less what others in public think and they continue to move forward and take the child to social outings despite the child's repeated protests or poor behavior. Second, not every child fits neatly into any one style of relating to others. All kids have good days and bad days. Finding a time to take him out to a play date may just be a matter of learning how to "read" your child to know when is the best time or day.

A major consideration with approach-avoidance conflict is that if parents are not careful, kids can and do begin to shape *a parent's* behavior. Parents can change their approach to the child (e.g., not encouraging the child to go out with others anymore) to keep the child, as well as siblings and themselves, comfortable. Thus, repeated "failure" and difficulty can be averted simply by staying in the comfort of your home, with your family. However, this approach only reinforces anxiety and it certainly does nothing to improve the child's current level of social functioning.

Even when parents are not around, the child may continue this pattern of interaction that results in anxiety and influences the behaviors of others. For example, peers may repeatedly initiate interactions and activities with the child while at school. The child in question, who is anxious and fearful of failing or "looking stupid," may reject the efforts and invitations of the other kids (another approach-avoidance example). The peers are doing the majority of the work and the child is essentially sabotaging their efforts by rejecting their repeated attempts to connect. Kids will eventually stop asking the child to play if their offers continue to be rejected or they receive no response.

Ambivalence

Ambivalence is a central characteristic of approach-avoidance conflict and is defined as a state of having simultaneous, conflicting feelings toward a person or thing. Stated another way, ambivalence is the experience of having thoughts and emotions that are both positive and negative, toward someone or something. I love the taste of chocolate, but I hate that it causes me to gain weight. Therefore, I stand in the candy aisle holding a chocolate bar debating whether or not I want to buy it. The expression, "sitting on the fence" is often used to describe the feeling of ambivalence.

Ambivalence is experienced as psychologically unpleasant when the positive *and* negative aspects of a subject are both present in a person's mind at the same time. This state can lead to avoidance or procrastination, or to deliberate attempts to resolve the ambivalence. When the situation does not require a decision, people experience less discomfort even when feeling ambivalent. An example would be the teen who acknowledges that social skills are important but nevertheless fails to engage in the necessary social skills training because his attitude is ambivalent.

Ambivalent attitudes may also be more susceptible to information or persuasion. If individuals strongly maintain that social skills are important, but feel ambivalent towards this issue, even trivial information could change their overall attitude. After hearing from a peer that a social group the peer attended was "stupid" and "a waste of time," the ambivalent teen might immediately decide that trying to improve social skills would be a waste of his time as well. Indeed, a person can successfully lessen his discomfort regarding the approach to others by avoiding social interactions or putting them off. However, we must be careful as "Five more minutes, please" becomes five more years rather quickly.

Overcoming Ambivalence

Using the **5R**'s of the Sōsh approach can help overcome ambivalence. The **5R**'s are the basis of the Sōsh approach to social skills development and help reveal the answers to the question of how to improve social skills. First, it is important to **Relax** initially and cope with the stress associated with the ambivalence or approach-avoidance conflict. Next, you need to think it through or **Reason** by considering all relevant perspectives related to the situation and determine how to approach a social interaction. Once ready to approach, utilize the strategies of connecting with others (finding common ground, conversation strategies, etc.) discussed in the **Relate** section. When engaged in the social interaction, consider the emotions involved (**Recognize**) and control your behaviors (**Regulate**) so that you do not negatively affect the situation or those around you. If, during the course of this process, you need a break to reenergize, then by all means take a break. Don't forget about the oxygen mask on the airplane! Just be sure that the breaks do not outnumber the opportunities, and also be sure to set a deadline for when to begin again.

When I'm working with families, one of my main talking points relates to the comfort associated with the current pattern of avoidance of anxiety. Avoidance only encourages solitary activities that, while providing immediate comfort, hinder social progress. While the initial attempts to encourage social exposure will be met with anxiety and perhaps even hostility, the child must continue to be encouraged and supported to pursue relationships outside of the family home.

Family Dynamics and Approach-Avoidance

I often complete a family genogram when working with the family of a child with social difficulties. A genogram is a pictorial display of a person's family relationships and medical history. It goes beyond a traditional family tree by allowing the user to visualize hereditary patterns and psychological factors that influence relationships within the family system. I find that there were often approach-avoidance conflicts in the families of parents, who now have a child with a social skills difficulty, when they were growing up. For instance, parents who grew up in homes where conflict was either avoided completely (i.e., "swept under the rug") or addressed with strong reactivity (resulting in "walking on eggshells") often find themselves approaching stress and conflict with their children in a similar fashion now that they are parents. Like many relationship patterns, the approach-avoidance conflict may be passed from generation to generation.

Family members profoundly affect each other's thoughts, feelings, and actions. Families solicit one another's attention, approval, and support and react to each other's needs, expectations, and distress. This results in the functioning of the family in an interdependent manner. Thus, a change in one family member's functioning changes the entire family dynamic. Families differ in terms of how much they influence one another, but some degree of influence among and between family members is always present.

When a family member becomes anxious, the anxiety can spread infectiously to other family members. One parent will often "jump in" to buffer the stress by accommodating the child's difficulties. The other parent may refer to this as "babying" or "coddling" the child. Although it is not always the mother who "jumps in," she is the person who generally spends the most time with the child and some additional accommodation from her is to be expected. Unfortunately for the mother (or any family member who is trying to alleviate the child's stress), the one accommodating the child literally "absorbs" the anxiety and becomes the family member most vulnerable to problems such as depression, anxiety, or physical fatigue and even pain. A vicious cycle may begin where the mother is fatigued because she is absorbing the anxiety, and as a result she lacks the energy to assist the child in their social development. If your family is already in the midst of absorbing the stress of one of its members, and it is taking a toll, you might consider consulting with a mental health professional. In addition to helping the family dynamic, this is useful for the child who may be the identified "patient" as it fosters a sense of collaboration among family members and diffuses the stress, so that the child is not left feeling that the family stress is his fault.

Parenting and Extended Family, Oh My!

Parenting is challenging. It requires consistency and communication with anyone who has an influential role in the child's upbringing. All too often, mothers and fathers enable their child's behavior in an effort to overcompensate for the child's difficulties or to maintain the peace in the family home. It is essential to be aware of our personal parenting dynamics and troubleshoot them as needed. For example, with a child who experiences a developmental delay (e.g., a speech delay), many parents feel badly for their child and therefore give in to their child's acting out behaviors. They assume, "Well, he can't talk so he must be frustrated and hitting is his way of telling others how upset he is."

The fact is that hitting is never acceptable regardless of a child's language delay, mobility issues, or whatever the "reason" may be. What might keep the peace in the short term only hurts the child's long-term development. For example, the child with the language delay likely will catch up and meet the expressive and receptive speech milestones of his peer group, but may continue to hit others. Now, he will require behavior modification. The peer group responds to his hitting by avoiding the child to prevent personal harm, or labeling him as the "bad" kid. The speech delay may have been resolved but the behavioral aggression is now more challenging to address given that the child is older, bigger, and stronger. Perhaps the peer group previously could not connect to the child because he was not speaking. Now that he is speaking, they cannot connect because he frightens them with his hitting behaviors and they avoid him.

If parents feel at a loss in their approach to parenting, I recommend parenting counseling to get away from the idea of "fixing" and instead provide coaching opportunities. Accomplishing goals may be more effective if the approach is modified and parents can be provided with a consistent approach regarding how they need to respond to the child. The family dynamics need to be explored as well because having a child with a developmental delay can and will affect a parent's ability to discipline effectively. Whether out of guilt, sympathy, pity, or concern that discipline will delay development further, many parents find themselves caught up in this dilemma and need assistance and perhaps "permission" to move forward with firm and consistent parenting approaches.

The stress of having a child who has some level of difficulty, whether it's a neurodevelopmental diagnosis or other challenge, is significant and can put strain on a marriage, especially if the parents are not in agreement regarding the child's diagnosis, delay, or the approach to take to help the child. The first way to insulate yourself and your spouse from marital stress related to the child is to communicate effectively. Establishing a parenting plan and adhering to it can help avoid "splitting." Splitting is a term used by some psychologists to refer to the process in which a child "plays" or attempts to turn one parent against another. The classic example is when the adolescent goes to one parent to ask to borrow the car and that parent says "No." The teen then goes to the other parent, without telling them about the "No" response, and asks again. When this parent says "Yes," the teen goes back to the first parent with this information, or just takes the car because, after all, one parent said "yes." Thus, it helps parents to be on the same page by establishing a consistent parenting approach in order to prevent conflict that tends to result from varying styles and approaches. The child is less likely to try to split when he observes an alliance between parents. Further, if your child has engaged in splitting in the past (or you want to avoid it altogether), then put any decision on hold until you can discuss it with your spouse. In the car example, the parent could have said, "I need to discuss your request for the car with your [mother/father] before giving you an answer."

Kids often try to rush this process by insisting they have to know *right now*, but enough exposure to your routine and process of addressing these types of questions will alert to the child to the ineffectiveness of this approach. Further, teaching a child to delay his gratification is important to his development. It also allows the child with some time to think about alternatives (e.g., who else could drive tonight?) if he is not granted immediate access to the car. If the question is a regular occurrence, such as borrowing the car on the weekends, then you will want to sit down as parents and determine what the family policy is for car use and explain this in advance to the child so that splitting is prevented in the future.

Self-Esteem and the "Pillars of Confidence"

Self-esteem is vulnerable throughout the lifespan but especially once children leave the "comfort bubble" of early childhood. Young children are surrounded primarily by their immediate family, who typically praise their children, getting the "best" out of them. Indeed, children often perform their "tricks" (e.g., singing, dancing, jumping) in the comfort of their living room and receive wild applause in exchange for their efforts. Eventually these children venture out of the safety of their home and "into the wild."

I liken the ability of the child to function best within the "comfort bubble" of home to Warner Bros. cartoons. There are a series of episodes that feature a frog who sings "Hello My Baby." A man stumbles across the frog, and the frog jumps out of a box with a top hat and a cane that he uses to dance as he loudly and confidently sings the song. The man visualizes the earning potential (graphically depicted over his head) associated with owning a dancing, singing frog. He reserves a theater and places the frog on the stage in front of a sold-out audience. The curtain rises and the frog looks at the audience, but he remains still on the floor. The audience leans forward in anticipation. The frog's only utterance is "ribbit." The man is devastated. As the curtain comes down, the frog begins to sing and dance again outside of the view of the crowd.

Kids typically "look good" at home with parents and siblings because the family accommodates them. Families learn to interact and react to the child in a very specific way so as to avoid conflict or strong reactions. Once we introduce the child into the real world, difficulties begin. Social skills difficulties, specifically, don't exist *in* the home because the child is not being asked to do anything outside of his comfort zone, or relate to anyone that he doesn't already know. Only when situations arise *outside* of the home in which the child must be socially flexible, reciprocal, and fluent in his interaction with people, do major difficulties arise. The good news is that once the initial stress associated with these difficulties is managed, the child has an incredible opportunity to practice a new set of reactions and interactions that exist in real world contexts. The world knows nothing of the child's history or what helps to keep him comfortable. Thus, the world is an "as is" entity and the child must learn to adjust, instead of everyone else adjusting to him. This adjustment can have an effect on self-esteem, and must be monitored closely.

Self-esteem often absorbs its first "insult" when the child is left somewhere other than the home and asked to navigate a new or different environment on his own. Preschool or kindergarten may be the first time that social skills difficulties are noted, especially if the child is a firstborn and there has been no previous basis for comparison within the family. Self-esteem generally doesn't experience its first *big* insult, however, until the first grade. This is because there is little feedback from adults or peers in preschool or kindergarten based on performance. Instead, the focus is on playing, and on practicing foundational skills. This is rapidly changing, though, as the demands upon younger children are increasing in school. As a result, I would expect younger children to experience more self-esteem challenges as these societal and school expectations continue to rise. Kindergarten teachers in Michigan have reported to me during the past several years that, during their kindergarten readiness evaluations, the primary concerns are the social and emotional development of the kids.

First grade is often when children begin to learn that they do not receive unconditional positive support and regard from all adults in their lives (as they have, up until now, from their parents). Everything they do is not earth-shattering, groundbreaking, and wonderful, as their loving and proud parents would have them to believe. The things a child does wrong or incorrectly need to be pointed out to him and corrected for learning to occur. This is when self-esteem initially begins to decline. Children eventually learn, however, that this feedback is intended to help them improve their knowledge and skill set and is not a repeated attempt to insult or hurt them. Then, as children enter the Catch-22 of social skills development (around approximately nine years of age) in which they desire social interactions, but also recognize they are having difficulties socially, another decline in self-esteem occurs.

The effect of "letting go" of a child into the real world is important in the child's development. Parents want their children to be self-assured. Enrolling a child in school (preschool or kindergarten) is the first time when parents don't have much, if any, control over who the child will meet or how he will be treated, or how he will treat others. Parents must simply wait and pick up the pieces and try to put on the best "poker face," listening with angst, guilt, and anger (among other emotions) as the child recounts being teased or feeling rejected earlier that day. The hope is that the child will remain open to discussing these things, but adult reactions to these stories influence the child's willingness to contine to share.

I recently listened to one of my colleagues recount how, when her son was younger (he is now a teenager), he came home one day and told her, "Johnny told me that he didn't want to be my friend!" She recalled how she bit her lip and was ready to give him a big hug as he was surely on the verge of tears. She put on her best "poker face" and asked her son, "What did you say?" Her son responded in a matter-of-fact tone, "I said, 'Who cares'!?"

Some kids are simply born with a "suit of armor" that can repel such comments, while others are devastated at the very thought of anyone not liking them. Self-esteem can deteriorate at school when a child has a difficult time with math, reading, friendships, or anything else that the child internalizes as making them "defective" or "flawed" in any way. In order to help support a child's self-esteem it is important to have an understanding of the construct itself. Self-esteem, was defined by William James (1890) one of the pioneers of the field of psychology, with the following equation: **Self-Esteem = Success/Pretensions** (or Success divided by Pretensions).

Pretensions are viewed as goals, purposes, or aims, whereas **Successes** constitute the *perception* of the attainment of those goals. Thus, we essentially decide on our own when we have achieved success based on expectations for that success. Self-esteem begins to suffer when an individual comes up short in his perception of reaching a particular goal, especially when the individual compares his achievement of a goal against the achievement of others. So, for the child who tells himself (or hears from his parents) that he *must* get straight "A's" and then gets a "B" in gym class, self-esteem has just taken a "hit." Whereas another child who really struggles in gym class and has lower or perhaps even more realistic expectations for success and eventually achieves a "B" in the class may experience no change, or perhaps even a rise in self-esteem.

The bottom line, which is as important for adults as it is for kids, is that we must have multiple "columns" or "pillars" of confidence to support our self-esteem. If *all* of our esteem depends upon how well we do in school, for example, and we do lousy on a particular test, then we are in emotional conflict with ourselves. This is why I strongly encourage kids to pursue a variety of interests beginning in the early elementary school years (in middle school at the very latest), even if they only end up liking a few things. I don't expect that they will like everything they try (or be good at everything), but having multiple interests can insulate them down the road if their participation in one those interests does not go well. Thus I recommend exposing the child to a variety of activities, with the expectation that the child choose one or two activities to engage in regularly outide of the home (e.g., Boy Scouts, swimming lessons) so as not to be overscheduled.

Returning to the discussion of pretensions, imagine that I enter a contest and win the opportunity to throw out the first pitch at a Major League Baseball game. I practice a little so that I don't embarrass myself on the big day. I step up on the mound, attempt my best wind up, and throw a wild pitch that sends the catcher scrambling and draws jeers from the crowd. It's all in good fun and I laugh it off. Why don't I hang my head and "beat myself up" about this? Why hasn't my self-esteem suffered? Well, for starters I am not a trained professional pitcher, so why should I be expected to throw an accurate pitch from that distance? But what if I were a professional ball player and I performed the same way? Then my self-esteem might be in jeopardy because my pretensions are different. I would have been *expected* to throw more accurately.

The young boy I discussed earlier with the "suit of emotional armor" responding with neutrality to a peer not liking him comes to mind. As a psychologist, my reaction to my wild pitch can safely be, "Who cares!?" There are other things I do well and my pretensions for throwing the ball well or accurately were low. As a result, not achieving success was okay. This is exactly why multiple pillars of support is essential for self-esteem. If my entire self-concept is tied up in how knowledgeable and helpful I am as a psychologist, and a child comes to see me to whom I can't seem to connect, then I run the risk of becoming overly critical of myself and questioning my competence. However, if I go home to my family that night and watch as my daughter and son greet me excitedly and play with me because they consider me to be a good father, I am reminded that there is more to me and my self-concept than what I do at work, or how well I perform while I am there.

Kids need to be reminded to find successes in what they do multiple times a day. It is the job of parents to increase the chances of them being able to accomplish this by encouraging their involvement in a range of activities that involve a variety of people. A bad day at school is only devastating when the pretensions of how school *should* go are set too high. Were there *any* good parts of your terrble day? Was it really a comprehensively bad experience *all* day? Teaching our kids to challenge their negativistic and all-or-nothing thinking may be the key to ensuring that they return to the situations that furstrated or upset them in order to try again. This work requires repetition, patience, and practice. Asking kids questions that challenge a black-and-white line of thinking provides modeling for how they can talk themselves out of a difficult emotional position in the future, and preserve their self-esteem.

The Trouble with Change

Human beings do not handle change well. In fact, we hate it. Change is difficult, complicated, and messy. We often view change as something difficult or unpleasant that we don't *want* to do but that we *need* to do. That being said, one of the most effective ways to evoke change in any aspect of our lives is to alter the way we think in order to change our behaviors. This is difficult to do. Changing our thinking patterns as adults can be very helpful (and is often necessary) when trying to assist a child with social skills development. While acknowledging that change *is* difficult, try to approach the change positively. What can be exciting about change is the opportunity to think differently. The adult's role is to help the child to see it this way. Use rewards to keep motivation going and don't forget to be creative. Use humor whenever possible, and have fun as you tailor your approach to suit the child's unique needs and level of development.

Behavioral interactions are one of many ways to help a child to change his thinking. It's the same phenomenon that occurs when you serve a child something for dinner and he rejects it. You might say in that instance, "Okay, if you don't like it, then I'll never serve that again." The child begins to think, "All I need to do to get what I want is to avoid what I don't want." This never gives the child an opportunity to truly think through his decision-making process. If the child always has an escape, he certainly won't learn to try new experiences. So, consider tolerating the conflict and encouraging the child to **Reason** or "think it through" (e.g., "Have you tried this food enough to really know whether or not you like it?"), rather than just responding based on habit or emotion. Also, remember to make changes gradually, as children are more open to take a small step as opposed to a big one. Using the food example as a guide, the parent might introduce one new food gradually along with the child's favorites and provide a reward for trying the new food. This is in contrast to refusing to offer the child his favorites and instead only offering several new foods that he is forced to try.

Pick Your Battles and Allow Time to Think

Choose your battles wisely. If the child is doing well in most areas of his life with the exception of eating habits, for example, then we might cut him a little more slack and work gradually to expand his eating habits. The Sōsh approach is flexible and encourages individuals to take it one step at a time. Choose one area to work on and practice the skill over a long enough period of time to master it. Also, be sure to pace yourself and monitor the child's energy level. Fatigue and frustration can defeat kids to the point of zero effort. Thus, choosing your battles with social skills intervention involves taking it one step at a time, and not trying to climb Mount Everest before you take a rock climbing class at your local community recreation center.

I recall one of my first jobs working at McDonald's cooking hamburgers. I was 15 years old, and it was a summer job. After my first day on the job I came home and told my parents, "I can't do this anymore. I want to quit." They listened and acknowledged and understood that I was frustrated, that I did not have a good first day, that it was a bad experience, and that the job did not seem like a good fit for me. But, they also said that in order to make a truly informed decision, I needed to put in at least one week's worth of work before we could revisit my request to quit. So, I agreed (thinking I would "serve my time" for the week and then quit), and I went back to work for another week. Ultimately, I ended up working there for the rest of the summer. What I didn't know at that time was that my parents were helping me carve out the necessary time to *think* my decision through, and to avoid making any decisions based on initial emotional response.

A good thing to remember is that it is very difficult for people to be both logical and emotional at the same time. These two brain systems compete with one another. This is one of the reasons why many states have a 72 hour waiting period before you can buy a firearm. The law is designed to allow a person to "cool off" if this is an emotional purchase (e.g., "I am so mad!"), and allow the logic (e.g., "If I shoot someone I will go to jail") to occur. Similarly, you need to allow the child enough time (the amount varies depending on the child) for the initial emotional reaction to subside before trying to talk it out or problem-solve.

Distractions: Screen Time

The American Academy of Pediatrics (AAP) guidelines recommend that parents limit a child's "screen time" (i.e., video games, computer, television) to one to two hours per day ***at most.*** An alternative that I have often recommended to families I work with is to limit screen time to one hour on school nights and two hours a day on weekends and holidays. My intention is not to make the child's life miserable (which they often accuse me of trying to do), but rather to create opportunities for relationships with people. Restricted screen time is recommended and intended to limit *noneducational* use of screens. Thus, watching movies, television, or playing video games would fall under the restriction guidelines of one to two hours per day. However, using the computer to research a report, reading an e-book on a portable device, or doing math drills online would not count toward the restricted time.

Video games are not social. Even if your child plays with a friend in the same room, or online, this is not a spontaneous and reciprocal social interaction. Indeed, if you turned off the video game and asked the two kids in the room to get a conversation going for more than a few minutes, they would inevitably become uncomfortable and want to discuss or return to playing the video game. Please don't misinterpret what I'm saying here. I think that some exposure to video games is actually a good thing. Especially from a social skills framework because many children, especially boys, love video games and thus talk about them with each other at school. Not knowing anything about these games can leave a person feeling left out. My concern with video games is that many children cannot limit the time they spend playing them and this can create considerable conflict between parents and children. It can also become a solitary (and sedentary) activity for the child that significantly interferes with social opportunities, and the development of social skills.

Although the strategies for how to wean a child from excessive video game usage vary from family to family, a few points of advice may provide a good start:

- Make conversation a priority in your home.
- Read to your children.
- Play with your children.
- Encourage active recreation.
- Get the TV sets, computers, and video game systems out of your children's bedrooms. It is not a good idea to have TVs and computers in bedrooms **at any age**, even if the child is younger and you think that it is harmless because they only look at children's websites, or you have an internet filter set up. The fact is, you are training their brain to want and need this technology available in their room, which will affect sleep habits as well as social interactions, especially with family members.

Children who excessively play video games or watch television tend to do so for a reason. Whether it is loneliness, social skills difficulties, anxiety, or depression, the use of video games and television viewing becomes self-medicating and a means to quickly pass the otherwise painful time spent thinking about reality. The strategies mentioned above are only a drop in the bucket if your child is experiencing social or emotional difficulties. If you are fortunate enough to be reading this while your child is still young, the best form of intervention is prevention. Start early and set those limits now while encouraging more appropriate use of your child's time. Get him involved in fun activities out of the home to keep him interested and active. If your child is already hooked on video games for excessive amounts of time, it may be worthwhile to seek a professional consultation to begin breaking the so-called video game "addiction," and develop a schedule to reduce his playing time and replace it with more productive activities.

I think about the state of Michigan, in which it seems to take about 30 minutes to get to many activities and locations outside your town or city. If, for example, you drive your child to swimming lessons to a location 30 minutes away, and you use a DVD system in your car, then your child has just watched one hour of screen time during this round trip, the recommended daily amount according to the Amercian Academy of Pediatrics. Thus, the remainder of the day should be filled with interactive, engaging, and imaginative activities that do not involve watching videos or television shows.

Screens in cars are often a sanity preserver for many families, but should really be reserved for long trips, no matter how much the child requests. If the child requests and gets to watch a DVD once, it becomes the standard for riding in the car. Further, if you think that this interest will only be associated with the car, think again. Kids who enjoy watching television and DVDs want to engage in this activity regardless of the location (i.e., car, living room, bedroom).

One way of avoiding incessant requests by the child to watch videos in the car is to establish rules in advance, discuss them with the child, and follow them. Having these rules established is especially important if you happen to be daring enough to purchase or lease a car with DVD screens built into the vehicle's headrests. My advice is to keep the DVD in the car turned off unless it's a trip over two to three hours long, and even then it should only be allowed for selected parts of the trip. The other option is to avoid the premium DVD car package with your new vehicle and use a portable system that attaches to headrests or sits on the child's lap so that it can be removed from the car during short in-town trips and reserved for longer trips, as recommended. Out of sight is not necessarily out of mind for kids who depend on screens for entertainment, but it sure is a lot easier to say "No" to a complaining child when the device is not even in the car! The same rules can be applied to the use of handheld video game systems.

Whatever happened to good old fashioned conversation while on car trips or a game of *Eye Spy*? Perhaps Mom or Dad are too busy on *their* phone or device to have a dialogue with the child. I must admit this is one of my pet peeves, especially when I see a parent pick a child up from school after not seeing them all day and they are on the phone instead of greeting the child and catching up on the day! It is essential to create a positive experience in the car with your kids by talking, playing games, and even listening to music and singing together. It is equally important to practice what you preach and limit your own screen time (e.g., how often you check your email or text on your phone in front of the child) as a parent if you are to limit the child's time. Finally, remember that modeling is a powerful force in the life of a child and when they see you worshipping your phone and ignoring their requests for attention, you are headed for trouble.

"Good" Screen Time and Creativity

Screens where there is interaction and more active attention, such as the Sōsh application, provide the necessary balance between a screen or interface that is familiar and attractive to the child, while at the same time coaching and encouraging social interaction, which is appealing to parents, teachers, therapists, and often to the peer group. Thus, Sōsh is designed to take advantage of the child's natural curiosity and interest in technology while promoting *active* participation in the real world rather than *passive* viewing on the couch where no social skills development can occur.

Occasionally I have the oportunity to meet a child in my private practice who has not succumbed to television and video games, and I must say that these are some of the most creative and social individuals that I have the opportunity to meet with in my work. Their brains are so full of ideas and creativity, and they are able to entertain themselves and create, rather than just absorbing what is presented to them. These are the kids who do not need the light up, noisy toys that do all the work for them.

I recently met a boy who does not have a television in his home and the creativity of this young man was unbelieveable. I am not suggesting that you strip all electronics from your home, or ban telvision or video games. I do, however, want to emphasize the importance of setting limits on viewing. Consider times in which you had no choice, like when you were on vacation at a relative's home or at a lakeside cottage and there was no video console. What happened to the child after he stopped complaining and accepted the need to figure out something else to do? If you allow a child enough time, you will be amazed at what his brain will come up with. It's refereshing to see a child who will create something out of what is available rather than a child who begs you to play a video game or complains of being "bored" because he requires constant video stimulation to be entertained. Remember when your kids were little and you spoiled them with tons of gifts on their birthday, or a holiday, only to see them experience more joy playing with the boxes, bubble wrap, or wrapping paper? Food for thought.

The Patience to Improve

Only one who devotes himself to a cause with his whole strength

and soul can be a true master. For this reason mastery demands <u>all</u> of a person.

~Albert Einstein

Very often I see books in my local bookstore that claim to be able to teach me how to "master" a skill in only ten days. There are even tutorials claiming to teach a skill in just a few hours. Pretty soon we'll be demanding to know how to do something in seconds. Unfortunately, the reality is there's only one approach to become good at social skills and it is outlined below:

- First, a child *can* learn some social skills by reading about them or listening to others who have good skills (e.g., parents, teachers, therapists), but for lifelong change to occur he needs to <u>use the skill</u>. This approach is consistent with the medical school teaching model of *See One, Do One, Teach One* that was described in the **Development** chapter, and which I have found to be the most effective way to learn social skills.

- Next, once the child is through the *Do One* stage with a particular social skill, he needs to perform the skills some <u>more</u>. At this point, he will begin to understand it, but he will also continue to be awful at it. This is not unique to a person struggling with social skills. Most new things that we try to do result in poor execution in the early stages. This stage of practice takes months and even years.

- Then, the child continues to practice and complete additional social skills exposure and practice. After a couple of *years*, the child will *begin* to get good at it. Notice the italics highlighting the fact that this will require years of commitment to improve. This is presented in the **Barriers** chapter because some people don't have the patience or persistence necessary to commit this kind of time and effort, for a variety of reasons (some of which may have been addressed throughout this chapter). Once he is good at it, he can begin to *Teach One* by coaching a peer or younger child who does not yet have this skill (although simpler skills that do not take years to master can be taught to others much sooner).

- Finally, practice social skills some more. We learn a lot from mistakes, so if the child can be encouraged to make mistakes in order to boost learning (and also to preserve self-esteem by giving permission to "mess up" in advance), he will soon improve from "Mediocre" to "Good" or even from "Good" to "Great." This is why it is especially important that you keep anxiety in check among all participants. Anxiety can cause kids to retreat from continued practice, especially if the results are not as immediate. If we can manage these feelings and acknowledge the time needed to improve, we can begin to see the expected gains and progress in social skills.

It takes anywhere from 6-10 years to get good at something, depending on how often and how much you do it. Some estimate that it takes 10,000 hours to master a skill, but I think it varies from person to person and depends on the skills of the person, among other factors. One thing is for certain: There is no one who is great at his or her profession who hasn't been doing it for at least 6 years; no designer, no programmer, no carpenter, no architect, no surgeon, no teacher, no musician, no artist--you get the point. I challenge you to name one. Most truly skilled practitioners have been doing it for over a decade, and are still looking to improve. Even so-called "overnight" sensations or success stories have been practicing in a basement or elsewhere for years before they were "discovered." Being good at anything takes desire, it takes drive, and it takes lots and lots of practice (and maybe even a little luck).

Think about it this way: Would you allow a surgeon to operate on you if he had only read about the procedure in a book or learned about it in a classroom? I doubt it. The same logic applies to social skills improvement. Individuals can read books and talk about social skills during therapy sessions, but until they are out and about practicing what they have been studying, they will not be good at it. Even the smartest aspiring surgeons in the classroom report that they didn't really learn until they were in the operating room with a skilled surgeon who was guiding them and coaching them *in the moment.*

The difficulty here is that we are targeting our social skills efforts in most cases to children. If the social "switch" does not turn on in the brain until age 9, then we still have good teaching years before age 18, correct? Not necessarily. There is a lot happening during these years of development that delays progress. Things may be on hold for a few years while your family regroups and you modify your strategy to meet the child's developmental needs. The child may not show real interest in socializing until they are college age. The main thing to remember is not to become discouraged, no matter how old the person is when they are ready to begin. If you are the parent of a child who does not decide until later in life that he wants some assistance to be more social, provide as much support as you can. You can assist him locating a specialist who can coach him on these strategies and provide encouragement.

Prior to a younger child's interest in improving social skills, parents are encouraged to provide the child with play dates, activities, and other social opportunities that serve as exposures for the child as well as opportunities for the parent to coach the child. This approach is especially important for kids who are in the latency stage of development (i.e., ages 6-9) where not much seems to be happening developmentally. These are typically kids who have an autism spectrum diagnosis and have completed early intervention that usually ends when they are 6 years old. Thus, before the "switch" turns on around their 9th birthday that internally motivates the child to desire more social skills, parents often try to locate groups and other social supports. Parents remain, however, the most important social coaches during this time. Thus, these parents must be willing to dedicate the necessary time, a couple of hours per day, to social skills coaching using the *See One, Do One, Teach One* approach in various social situations and with a variety of kids with whom the child can interact.

Review this chapter again if you think that something other than development is interfering with the desire to get started. Perhaps the child is ready but is experiencing anxiety or is "numbing" or self-medicating his feelings (and thus stalling progress) by escaping into video game play or some other solitary activity. If you are "stuck" then the guidance of a trained developmental specialist is essential to move things along. Once you are ready to begin (or pick up where you left off), remember to have fun, don't take yourself too seriously, keep the expectations realistic, and relax.

When the world says, "Give up,"
Hope whispers, "Try it one more time."
~Author Unknown

Beware of the Self-Fulfilling Prophecy

A self-fulfilling prophecy is a prediction (by yourself or someone else) that ultimately becomes true by the very terms of the prophecy. An example is the child who falsely believes he will fail a test and begins to fear failing, then does actually fail the test. Self-fulfilling prophecies are commonly experienced among children with social skills difficulties. Many self-fulfilling prophecies can begin early in life as people tend to put children in roles. We may say, "Oh well, she's just shy," or "She's really outgoing, she's going to be a performer." "He's going to be a lawyer because he argues a lot" or whatever the example might be. You probably can think of several of these "predictive" phrases for your kids. As much as possible, parents should avoid putting these roles onto children.

If we are approached by parents, peers, or teachers in ways that suggest we struggle in certain areas, or need help with certain skills; we can expect to approach these areas with a degree of trepidation that may reduce our effectiveness, thus creating a self-fulfilling prophecy.

Thus, if the world is always approaching us as if we are struggling or can't do something, then eventually we will behave as if the world is right. Remember to keep interactions positive and praise or reward any behaviors that you would like to see more of from the child.

Key Points

- When setting goals, it is vital for children and parents to keep expectations realistic. Start small. There is no drive-thru, magical, one-size-fits-all, "happy pill" approach to address social difficulties.

- Kids with social difficulties may use the same strategies repeatedly, even though they are not working. Although moving from strategy to strategy too quickly is troublesome, recognizing when something is not working (perhaps the bar has been set too high) and making the necessary changes are essential.

- Parenting is challenging. It requires consistency and communication with anyone who has an influential role in the child's upbringing. All too often, mothers and fathers enable their child's behavior in an effort to overcompensate for the child's difficulties or to maintain peace in the home. It is essential to be aware of our personal parenting dynamics and troubleshoot them as needed.

- Choose your battles wisely. The Sōsh approach is flexible and encourages individuals to take it one step at a time. Choose one area to work on and practice the skill over a long enough period of time to master it. Also, be sure to pace yourself and monitor the child's energy level. Fatigue and frustration can defeat kids to the point of zero effort.

Conclusion

Throughout this book you have been introduced to the Sōsh approach to improving social skills for children and adolescents. Although these strategies are targeted primarily toward children and teens with neurodevelopmental disorders; young adults, adults, and individuals with no formal diagnosis can also benefit from using the Sōsh approach. Indeed, I see many families with a variety of concerns in my clinical practice and I utilize these strategies to help them (and their child) reach their goals.

Social skills are an important and complex part of development and can have a profound effect on a child's life. Improvements are certainly attainable, provided you are willing to work hard. Successful intervention requires an understanding and implementation of the "**5 R's**" of Sōsh: **Relate** (Connect with Others), **Relax** (Reduce Stress), **Regulate** (Manage Behaviors), **Reason** (Think it Through) and **Recognize** (Understand Feelings). These categories serve as a guide to facilitate and improve social skills.

With the strategies presented throughout this book in mind, you can begin to formulate small goals with the child while keeping expectations reasonable. Take small, manageable steps initially and be careful to walk that tightrope between challenging the child and making him overly anxious. There will be roadblocks along the way which will require flexibility in your approach. There will also be success, which will be worthy of celebration. As progress is made, check in with the child to see how he feels about the process and the progress he is making. Finally, seek the expertise of a child development specialist, especially during times in which the child seems stuck, or if momentum stalls.

The most rewarding times in our lives typically occur as the result of hard work. The process of improving social skills goals is no exception. The goal of Sōsh is to make this process a little more comfortable and manageable for all involved.

I wish you and your child the best as you embark on this challenging, yet rewarding journey toward improved social skills. One of the most gratifying aspects of my work with children and families is hearing success stories that are a result of using the Sōsh approach. To all of the parents and adults who are a positive influence in the life of a child, I thank you for all that you do and I sincerely hope that the strategies outlined in this book bring you and your family much success.

Too often we give our children answers to remember

rather than problems to solve.

~Roger Lewin

Bibliography

Beck, J. (1995). *Cognitive therapy: Basics and beyond.* New York: Guilford Press.

Bellini, S., Peters, J. K., Benner, L., & Hopf, A. (2007). A meta-analysis of school-based social skills interventions for children with autism spectrum disorders. *Remedial and Special Education, 28*(3), 153-162.

Bishop, S. R., Lau, M., Shapiro, S. L., Carlson, L., Anderson, N. D., Carmody, J. (2004). Mindfulness: A proposed operational definition. *Clinical Psychology: Science and Practice, 11*, 230–241.

Blumenthal, J. A., Babyak, M. A., Doraiswamy, M., Watkins, L., Hoffman, B. M., Barbour, K. A., Herman, S., Craighead, W. E., Brosse, A. L., Waugh, R., Hinderliter, A., Sherwood, A. (2007). Exercise and pharmacotherapy in the treatment of major depressive disorder. *Psychosomatic Medicine, 69*(7), 587-596.

Boles, R., & Bowers, M. (2003). *Group check-in and group therapy techniques and approaches within the elementary therapeutic classroom.* Unpublished Manuscript.

Brown. K. W., & Ryan, R. M. (2003). The benefits of being present: Mindfulness and its role in psychological well-being. *Journal of Personality and Social Psychology, 84*, 822-848.

Brown, S., & Vaughan, C. (2010). *Play: How it shapes the brain, opens the imagination, and invigorates the soul.* New York: Penguin.

Burns, D. (1999). *Feeling good: The new mood therapy revised and updated.* New York: Harper Collins.

Davis, S. F., & Palladino, J. J. (2000). *Psychology* (3rd ed.). Upper Saddle River, NJ: Prentice-Hall, Inc.

Dawson, P., & Guare, R. (2009). *Smart but scattered.* New York: Guilford Press.

Eddy, J. M., Reid, J. B., & Curry, V. (2002). The etiology of youth antisocial behavior, delinquency, and violence and a public health approach to prevention. In M. R. Shinn, H. M. Walker, & G. Stoner (Eds.), *Interventions for academic and behavior problems II: Preventive and remedial approaches* (pp. 27-52). Bethesda, MD: National Association of School Psychologists.

Erickson, E. (1963). *Childhood and society* (2nd ed.). New York: Norton.

Faber, A., & Mazlish, E. (1999). *How to talk so kids will listen and listen so kids will talk.* New York: Harper Collins.

Forehand, R., & Long, N. (2010). *Parenting the strong-willed child: The clinically proven five-week program for parents of two- to six-year-olds* (3rd ed). New Jersey: McGraw-Hill.

Gershoff, E. T. (2008). *Report on physical punishment in the United States: What research tells us about its effects on children.* Columbus, OH: Center for Effective Discipline.

Jacobson, E. (1938). *Progressive relaxation.* Chicago: University of Chicago Press.

James, W. (1890). *Principles of psychology.* New York: Henry Holt.

Krasny, L., Williams, B. J., Provencal, S., & Ozonoff, S. (2003). Social skills interventions for the autism spectrum: Essential ingredients and a model curriculum. *Child and Adolescent Psychiatric Clinics of North America, 12*(1), 107-122.

Lewin, K. (1935). *A dynamic theory of personality*. New York: McGraw-Hill.

Lyubomirsky, S. (2008). *The how of happiness*. Penguin: New York.

Matson, J. L., Matson, M. L., & Rivet, T. T. (2007). Social-skills treatments for children with autism spectrum disorders. *Behavior Modification, 31*(5), 682-707.

McFall, R. (1982). A review and the reformulation of the concept of social skills. *Behavioral Assessment, 4*, 1-33.

Mehrabian, A. (1981). *Silent messages* (2nd ed.). Belmont, California: Wadsworth Publishing Company.

Moskowitz, G. B. (2005). *Social cognition*. New York: The Guilford Press.

Phelan, T. (2003). *1-2-3 magic* (3rd ed.). Glen Ellyn, Illinois: Parent Magic, Inc.

Piaget, J. (1952). *The origins of intelligence in children*. Margaret Cook (Trans.). New York: International Universities Press.

Rao, P. A., Beidel, D. C., & Murray, M. J. (2008). Social skills interventions for children with Asperger's syndrome of high-functioning autism: A review and recommendations. *Journal of Autism and Developmental Disorders, 38*(2), 353-361.

Russ, S. (2004). *Play in child development and psychotherapy: Toward empirically supported practice*. New Jersey: Lawrence Erlbaum Associates.

Selman, R. L. (1971). Taking another's perspective: Role-taking development in early childhood. *Child Development, 42*, 1721-1734.

Sherif, M., Harvey, O. J., White, B. J., Hood, W. R., & Sherif, C. W. (1961). *Intergroup conflict and cooperation: The Robbers Cave experiment*. Norman: University of Oklahoma Book Exchange.

Steele, M. (2011, January 4). Michigan middle school tests single-sex classes. *Detroit News*. Retrieved February 17, 2011, from http://www.news.yahoo.com.

Stone, C. A. (1993). What is missing in the metaphor of scaffolding. In E.A. Foreman, N. Minick, & C.A. Stone (Eds.), *Contexts for learning: Sociocultural dynamics in children's development*. New York: Oxford Press.

Straus, M. A. (1994). *Beating the devil out of them: Corporal punishment in American families*. Lanham, MD: Lexington Books.

Straus, M. A., & Paschall, M. J. (2009). Corporal punishment by mothers and development of children's cognitive ability: A Longitudinal study of two nationally representative age cohorts. *Journal of Aggression, Maltreatment, and Trauma, 18*(5), 459-483.

Vitaro, F., Brendgren, M., Larose, S., & Tremblay, R. E. (2005). Kindergarten disruptive behaviors, proactive factors, and educational achievement by early adulthood. *Journal of Educational Psychology, 97*, 617-629.

Vygotsky, L. S. (1978). *Mind in society: The development of higher psychological processes*. Cambridge, MA: Harvard University Press.

White, S. W., Keonig, K., & Scahill, L. (2007). Social skills development in children with autism spectrum disorders: A review of the intervention research. *Journal of Autism and Developmental Disorders, 37*, 1858-1868.

Wright, P. W. D., & Wright, P. D. (2007). *Wrightslaw: Special education law* (2nd ed.). Williamsburg, VA: Harbor House Law Press, Inc.

The Sōsh™ Mobile Application

The Sōsh™ mobile application was designed to assist individuals with social skills difficulties by putting the "**5R's**" to use in their everyday environments. It is designed to work with and for individuals when they need it the most: *In the Moment.* Developed by two psychologists, the Sōsh mobile application contains the critical elements that individuals need to improve their social skills. Whereas other social skills tools or strategies are commonly used in superficial settings (a therapy group, at home, in a therapist's office), this application can be carried with the individual and utilized in those real life social situations when questions arise.

The portability of the mobile application makes the intervention especially powerful and consistent with research findings about the importance of real world practice and intervention. The Sōsh application is comprehensive, customizable, user friendly, and intuitive. It is a teacher, therapist, parent, and coach all in the palm of your hand. Sōsh can (and should) be used in all settings of your day. The more time you spend with others, the more powerful this application becomes. If you are willing to put in the time and effort, Sōsh will help you accomplish your social goals.

For more information, visit: **www.mysosh.com**